Jinny Beyer's OLOR

CONFIDENCE *for*

QUILTERS

THE QUILT DIGEST PRESS
NTC/Contemporary Publishing Company

Acknowledgments

A very special thank you to The Quilt Digest Press, who gave me the opportunity and inspiration to write this book; to Dan Ramsey, who created the illustrations; to Hans Andress and Jill Johnson who worked with me on the fabric designs; to Rick Cohan, president of RJR Fashion Fabrics; and to the quilters whose work adorns the pages—Jeff Bar- tee, Darlene Christopherson, Barb Celio, Loanne Hamje, Jennifer Heffernan, Kay Lettau, Robin Morrison, Jay Romano, Kathy Light Smith, Toni Smith, Kay Sorensen, and Judy Spahn. Thanks also to Nancy Bruning, Leonore Par- ham and Bonnie Stratton; and to all my students who have continually given me support and inspiration.

Editorial and production direction by Bill Folk.
Production management by James Nelson.
Editing by Nancy Bruning. Copy editing by Janet Reed.
Cover copy by Sharon Gilbert.
Book design by Kajun Graphics, San Francisco.
Cover design by Jinny Beyer and Kajun Graphics.
Diagrams and illustrations by Dan Ramsey.
Photography by Sharon Risedorph, San Francisco.
Typographical composition by DC Typography, San Francisco.
Printed in Hong Kong.

Library of Congress Cataloging-in-Publication Data

Beyer, Jinny.
   [Color confidence for quilters]
   Jinny Beyer's color confidence for quilters.
      p. cm.
   Includes bibliographical references and index.
   ISBN 0-913327-39-5
   1. Quilts—Technique.   2. Color guides.   I. Title.
NK9104.B48   1992
746.9'7—dc20   92-24025
                                         CIP

Now published by NTC Publishing Group under ISBN 0-8442-2639-4

Published by The Quilt Digest Press,
a division of NTC Publishing Group
4255 West Touhy Avenue
Lincolnwood (Chicago), Illinois 60646-1975, U.S.A.
Printed in Hong Kong
7 8 9 0 WKT 9 8 7 6

To the memory of Michael Kile—
his pursuit of excellence has left a lasting mark.

CONTENTS

8   Introduction

12   About This Book

Chapter 1:
Creating Your Master Palette

14   How the Master Palette Concept Evolved

15   The Three Key Ingredients

15   *Shading*

15   *The Deep Dark*

15   *The Accent*

16   Why Make a Master Palette?

16   EXERCISE 1: Creating Your Master Palette

16   STEP 1. *Match the Color Swatches*

16   STEP 2. *Cut the Fabric Swatches*

17   STEP 3. *Find Colors to Fill the Gaps*

17   STEP 4. *Prepare a Board for Your Palette*

17   Shading the Swatches

17   STEP 5. *Sort the Swatches into Groups*

18   STEP 6. *Shade the Swatches Within Color Groups*

18   STEP 7. *Link the Color Groups Together*

20   STEP 8. *Work Through Possible Problems*

24   STEP 9. *Check the Shading*

24   STEP 10. *Add Fabrics from Your Collection*

Chapter 2:
Experimenting with Color
Combinations from the Master Palette

25   EXERCISE 2: Consider the Possibilities

26   It's All Relative

26   The Importance of Shading

26   Background Colors

27   Shading Two Colors

34   How Does Taste Fit In?

34   Shading Pale Colors Together

38   Working with Loose Swatches

39   EXERCISE 3: Shading Two Colors Together

40   Shading More Than Two Colors Together

41   EXERCISE 4: Shading Three or More Colors Together

42   Monochromatic Quilt Color Schemes

48   EXERCISE 5: Working with a Monochromatic Color Scheme

48   Proportion of Color and Value

Chapter 3:
Using Prints for Visual Texture

53   A Variety of Prints

54   Seeing in Black and White

55   EXERCISE 6: How Much Variety in Your Prints?

60   Avoiding Common Mistakes with Multi-Color Prints

Chapter 4:
Using Fewer Fabrics Versus Many Fabrics

63   The Advantages of Using Many Fabrics

66   Paring a Palette of Many Colors Down to a Few

67   STEP 1. *Choose Your Colors and Shade Them Together*

69   STEP 2. *Evaluate and Adjust Your Colors*

69   STEP 3. *Eliminate Colors*

69   EXERCISE 7: Selecting Fewer Colors from a Larger Palette

Chapter 5:
Designing a Palette to Coordinate with a Multi-Color Print

72   The Deep Dark—Easy to Miss

72   Theme Print Fabric as Guide, Not "God"

74   The Three Types of Coordinating Palettes

75   From the Expanded Palette to the Chosen Few

76   STEP 1. *Match the Colors*

76   STEP 2. *Shade the Colors*

76   STEP 3. *Eliminate Exact Matches*

77   STEP 4. *Work with Various Combinations*

82   Quilts Made Using Theme Print Fabrics

82   *Midnight Star* Series

90   *Rolling Star* Series

97   *Hound's Tooth Square* Quilt

100   EXERCISE 8: Coordinating Fabrics with Theme Prints

100   STEP 1. *Select a Print*

100   STEP 2. *Match the Colors*

100   STEP 3. *Shade the Colors*

100   STEP 4. *Pare Down the Colors*

100   STEP 5. *Find Fabrics for the Palette*

Chapter 6:
Palette Practice with Quilts

101   Designing and Making a Quilt

101   STEP 1. *Select a Quilt Pattern*

101   STEP 2. *Find a Unit*

102   STEP 3. *Design in Black and White*

104   STEP 4. *Plan the Size of the Quilt*

104   STEP 5. *(Optional) Draft the Pattern and Make the Templates*

104   STEP 6. *Create a Palette of Colors*

104   STEP 7. *Gather the Fabrics*

105   STEP 8. *Place the Colors Within the Quilt*

105   The Quilt Patterns

106   *Patterns Based on the 60° Diamond: Four Variations*

118   *Building Blocks: Four Variations*

125   *Rolling Star: Three Variations*

129   Enjoy Your New Color Confidence

130   Suggestions for Teachers

130   Teaching the Exercises

132   Classes in Basic Color Confidence

133   Palette Practice with Quilts

133   Resources

134   About Jinny Beyer

135   Paper Swatches and Sample Master Palettes

INTRODUCTION

I can still picture Miss Newton, my third grade teacher. She was old. Very old. We all thought she must be at least 100. She was also very crabby.

At the time, my two favorite colors were pink and purple. Whenever I would get a new box of crayons I would open them and marvel at the nice points and at how pretty they all looked standing proudly side by side in the box. Within no time my pink and purple crayons would be almost stubs while most of the others still had sharp points. Everything I colored had to have pink and purple in it . . . lots of pink and purple.

One day as I was at my desk, hunched over my coloring, loving the way the pink and purple played against each other on the page, I felt a heavy shadow behind me. I stole a glance over my shoulder and who should be looming over me with her gray hair swept up in a tight bun, black dress with the little white collar, black pointy laced shoes, stooped back, and stern look—who but Miss Newton, staring down at my picture. I slumped a little in my chair, hoping she would walk past me, but she whipped her hand out and grabbed my pink and purple crayons. Then, in her high-pitched cackley voice she screamed loud enough for the whole class to hear, "You always color everything pink and purple! Why do you always color everything pink and purple? Pink and purple don't go together! I don't ever want to see you using pink and purple together again!" With that she marched up to the front of the room, snapped in half the stubs of my two crayons and threw them in the trash bin.

For years thereafter whenever I would color something I would look at the pink and purple crayons, longing to use them in harmony, but would pass them by and go on to others as those cackling words echoed in my head: "Pink and purple don't go together!" Now, many years later, every time I boldly put pink and purple, red and purple, or fuchsia and purple in a quilt, I think of Miss Newton. I'm thankful that I am no longer fearful, as I was for years, that the colors I put together might not be "right." I'm also thankful that I finally feel liberated and confident enough about my color decisions to not be intimidated or influenced by what someone else thinks or says I should or should not do.

I am no good with color." I hear this phrase over and over in quilt shops, classes, or club meetings. Making color decisions is an important part of every aspect of our lives, yet it is something that is very intimidating to many people. What is it about color that affects everyone in such a way? What is it that caused so many people to run to "have their colors done" a few years ago and then never buy any article of clothing that did not exactly match the few swatches that the colorist gave them?

Why are we so insecure about by our own decisions of what colors we look good in that we let a total stranger tell us what colors we should wear? Why are we so anxious to let a shop owner tell us what colors and fabrics to pick for a quilt? Because we lack color confidence!

Perhaps we all had our own Miss Newtons in our childhood. The aura of the color wheel looms over us like a heavy shadow. We need to totally understand traditional color theory in order to be able to work with the wheel comfortably. As a result we feel constrained by what we think the color wheel dictates, instead of experimenting or trying different things.

It is important to follow your own instincts where colors are concerned and not get hung up on other people's "rules" about what colors can and cannot be used together. I once taught a class where someone had five coordinated prints containing four different colors that had been carefully chosen for a quilt. When I suggested that perhaps the addition of another color might be a nice spark, she said "Oh, but my quilt teacher said that we can only use four colors in a quilt."

How many colors would you say are in my quilt *Borealis*, shown on page 67? At first glance you think of purple and red. But if you isolate individual colors you could add black, green, burgundy, lavender, gray, blue, periwinkle, rose, . . . and on and on. Where does one color end and another begin? How do you distinguish one color from the next? When is the line drawn? At what point does red cease to be red and turn into burgundy? When does a gray-blue cease to be blue and turn into gray?

It is very fortunate for me that I began quiltmaking while living in India, isolated from anyone else who was making quilts and thereby forced to choose the colors that I liked, not those someone else might have suggested. With very little confidence in my own creative ability at that time, it would have been very easy for me to let others suggest color and fabric combinations. My first quilt was a *Grandmother's Flower Garden* (see illustration 1). The only pattern or instructions available to me in India was a black and white "Aunt Martha" pamphlet (Aunt Martha pamphlets were one of the few resources for patterns or literature available to quilters in the early 1970s), which gave the hexagon shape and a sample layout. Nothing was mentioned about what colors to use. It is certain that if I had been living in the United States and was associating with longtime quilters, I would have wanted to do what was "right." In 1972 most quilting was still very traditional and someone probably would have told me that when you make a *Grandmother's Flower Garden* quilt the center hexagon is always yellow, the surrounding hexagons are flower colors, and the background is white. That was the traditional way to make the design in the 1930s, 1940s, and 1950s and I would have dutifully made the quilt the way it was "supposed" to be done. But, you see, I didn't *know* that was the way the pattern should be made and the one thing that influenced the choices of color for my first quilt was a negative one.

Just prior to my decision to begin a quilt, some women in the American community in New Delhi decided to try their hand at making a quilt for a raffle. Having grown up with no quilts, nor having seen many during my lifetime, I did not know how quilts were "supposed" to look. In fact my major experience with anything quilted was mattress pads. Therefore upon seeing the raffle quilt on display (it was a white background with flowers appliquéd onto it and cross-hatch quilting throughout) I thought it looked like a mattress pad with flowers stuck onto it. Please don't get me wrong. Today I fully appreciate white on white quilts and intricate quilting designs, but to my inexperienced eye the quilt read "mattress pad." My next thought was that if I *ever* made a quilt, I didn't want anyone to think that I had bought a mattress pad and "doctored it up."

It was this experience that made me want to get as far from a mattress pad as possible and prompted me to select the deep rich muted colors of the hand-printed Indian cottons for my first quilt, not knowing that those colors were very different from what was being done at that same time in my home country. I was simply making a quilt to satisfy myself and using colors I liked. Upon returning home I joined a quilt group. When I showed my *Grandmother's Flower Garden* quilt for the first time, people were very complimentary about the colors. "How different your colors are . . . what a great sense of color you have." Those colors were so different from the ones being used in quilts made in the States in 1972. The praise I received for my quilt raised my confidence level enough that I continued to explore quilting and color, and my interest in designing my own color combinations and quilts, rather than copying what someone else had already done, grew.

However, my insecurity returned a few months later during one of our monthly quilt club meetings. The program chairman asked for volunteers to conduct programs for future meetings. Someone spoke up with "Jinny does such a good job of putting colors together, why don't we have her do a program on color?" Everyone else joined in and said they liked the idea and before I knew what had happened I had agreed to do the next month's program. Well, for the rest of the meeting I sat there *dying*. Why had I agreed to do it? What would I say? How could I possibly talk about

ILLUSTRATION 1: Grandmother's Flower Garden, *1972.*
First quilt made by Jinny Beyer.

color to other people when I didn't know anything about it myself?

After the meeting another member came up to me (I knew she had been to art school, and I was more than a little intimidated by her) and said, "Your program can be so exciting! You can make a color wheel with fabric and explain color theory as it applies to prints!" Is *that* what they want me to do? I went home in a state of panic, ran to the trash and rescued the new schedule of classes that had come that day from the local junior college. Poring through the bulletin, I hoped to find a color theory class that would start right away. There was nothing! The next morning I called the university to see if there was a class on color theory to take. There was, but it would cost $1200 to enroll as a part-time student, and it wouldn't start for three weeks. Next I went to the library and checked out every book on color that was there.

After a couple of days of trying to make sense out of primary, tertiary, binary, tone, shade, tint, complement, triad, and so on, and how they all related to each other, I finally sat back and realized, "They don't want me to talk about what I will learn in a crash course on color theory in the next month; they want to know how *I* work and how *I* approach color." Pushing the books aside, I went to my quilting projects and began to try to analyze my work. I was pleased with some of my patchwork projects and displeased with others. In some projects I had changed many colors until I was finally satisfied; others had seemed beyond redemption and were completely discarded. What was different about the various ones?

Preparing for that first program twenty years ago forced me to try to explain what I did instinctively. My color system was beginning to evolve. The more I taught, the more people asked me to teach my ideas on color, and the harder I tried to understand what to me was successful, what was not, and why.

A few years ago while planning the program for my annual Hilton Head Seminar, several of my colleagues said it was time for me to finally develop a program on

formal color theory that could be worked into the Seminar theme. I balked. How would it be possible to teach formal color theory when that isn't how I work? They told me I *did* work that way, but just didn't know it. So why, I asked, couldn't others work the way I did? If I still felt intimidated by traditional color theory, others must too. There had to be a way to teach others how color worked for *me*. Finally a series of exercises evolved, and more importantly, with the exercises came a way to explain how I work in simple, practical terms. My own way of working with color became more focused as well. I used to begin a quilt, study the first few blocks, realize something was missing, make changes back and forth and finally, after a lot of trial and error, be satisfied with the end product. Now, using the same exercises I have developed for classes and explain in this book, I create color palettes before starting a quilt. Since formalizing the system I have not once changed a color in a quilt after starting it, whereas previously I was constantly making color changes. The palette, created in advance, works!

When I began drafting my own patterns for quilt-making many years ago, it seemed there had to be a nonmathematical way to do it. I worked until I figured a way that seemed so much easier than formulas, algebra, and complex drafting tools. Just as my way of drafting geometric designs for quilts is through a practical, rather than mathematic approach, my way of working with colors is through a practical, rather than theoretical approach. I can probably figure out how to draft almost any geometric design, yet high school geometry (which I almost failed) is as far as my math education has gone. Likewise I have yet to take that color theory course but feel that the years spent teaching and making quilts have forced me to see color relationships, and has led me finally to a system that approaches color use from a simple, easy to grasp way. This book will help others who are not ready for formal color theory, color terms, and color wheels to learn my simple system and will give them the confidence to choose colors boldly.

ABOUT THIS BOOK

As we perform various tasks year after year, the way we perform those tasks varies over time. Everything we experience in life builds upon previous experiences to influence the way we think, respond, react, and create at any one time. My approach to color today is much different than it was ten years ago, and yours probably is too. I have many of the same ideas and treat color in quilts in much the same way, but through teaching, designing, and quiltmaking, I have expanded my ideas and have become much more confident in how I approach color in my own work and in how I teach my approach to others.

The color system that has developed over the last several years and that I explain in this book is based on using a master palette of fabric colors that span the spectrum. The master palette you create by following the instructions in this book will be *your* tool for color choices for all of your future quilting projects.

Chapter 1 takes you step by step through the process of creating your master palette. The ideal is for you to create one using all your own fabrics. You may already have most of the colors for the palette in your own fabric collection; feel free to fill in any gaps with the paper swatches reproduced in this book. Alternatively, you may choose to create your entire palette with the paper swatches or with one of the other color aids mentioned in the Resources section.

The master palette is your individual reference tool. Once the palette is created it will serve many functions. It will help you to follow and understand the exercises presented in each chapter; it will help you to determine where color gaps are in your own fabric collection; and it will serve as a guide to help you create individual palettes for specific quilts. Through the creation of this palette you will learn how the three ingredients that I feel are the foundation for a successful color scheme work. These ingredients are: **shading** (having several shades of each of the colors and then shading them together), the **deep dark** (a color darker in depth than the general range of other colors), and the **accent** (a color brighter than the range of other colors).

These three ingredients, no matter which colors are chosen, are the foundation of my color system. Until recently I always told students in my classes about them, expecting the students, with that simple explanation, to understand everything about my color system. But everyone, including me, needs some practical application of general principles to really believe in them, to gain insight, and to feel comfortable with them. That practical application for me came from making scores of quilt blocks and a couple of dozen quilts, but often changing some of the fabrics because the color didn't look just right. I was always pleased with the end result, but the process of changing colors and taking apart fabric pieces was at times quite frustrating.

It wasn't until that Hilton Head Seminar a few years ago where everyone was asking for "more on color" that I finally forced myself to try to develop some practical exercises for the participants. It was then that the whole color system I had been working with for years finally came together in a neat package, easy to explain and—most important—easy for others to grasp. I find it exciting that I now have a better understanding of color use in my own work and can explain it more easily to others. Even more exciting has been watching the faces of the students as they leave class after they have worked out the exercises. They beam and leave saying, "I feel so much more confident about color now!"

You too can feel more confident about color! Your own instincts are important. Trust them. What looks good to you and what does not is all a part of what makes up your personal style. Work through the exercises in this book. Don't just read the information and think you understand. It won't really hit home until you go through your own fabrics, do the exercises, and make a practical application of the material set forth here.

After creating your master palette you will learn how to create countless color schemes just by taking small sections of the palette, or by rearranging portions of it. You will learn how to pare a larger palette of colors down to just a few, how to work with many different types of prints to add a unique "texture" to your projects, and how to select the perfect color scheme to complement a large print fabric, wallpaper, upholstery, or other type of "theme" print.

This book will help you to gain confidence in choosing colors for any project. But in chapter 6, Palette Practice with Quilts, I have selected several patterns for those people who don't yet have a specific quilt in mind but are eager to begin. And if you are a quilt teacher, you will find it easy to use the lesson plans in the last chapter to help your students gain confidence in their color choices for quilts.

Chapter **1** CREATING YOUR MASTER PALETTE

How the Master Palette Concept Evolved

When I began teaching classes on color many years ago, I explained to the students about the need for shading colors together and the importance of the accent and deep dark colors. They were told to bring swatches of many different fabrics in their chosen color scheme to class and during class they were to shade their fabrics together. I realized this didn't work well, however, because they didn't have all of the necessary shades or the color groups to do this.

So I developed an exercise to be done in class where the students would work with colored swatches that *I* gave them. They could then relate those swatches to their own fabrics, using my swatches to fill the gaps of their missing colors. This still didn't work completely. The problem was that I couldn't find all of the necessary colors in printed fabrics. The only way I could find colors that spanned the spectrum was to use solid colored fabrics, and even then I had to purchase those solid colors from shops all over the country because they came from many different manufacturers.

For several years my students used these solid colored swatches (approximately 100) for the color exercises, and they were pleased and excited about the color combinations they were able to develop. However, the students became increasingly frustrated when, after developing their exciting color schemes, they could not always find printed fabrics in colors that matched the solids they had used in the exercises. For those wanting to make their quilts with solid colors, the task was a little easier, because they could eventually find those colors.

One day I walked into a comprehensive craft store and had a sudden thought. I looked at the wall containing embroidery floss and perle cotton. The hanks of thread were arranged by color and the wall *glowed* with the richness of color; the brighter colors, duller ones, and darker ones projected a harmonious impact. Next I saw hundreds of colored pencils grouped by color. Paints abounded in every color imaginable. I picked up a Pantone book containing standard printing colors. Then my eyes went to the wall containing bolts of cotton fabric. Something was missing. While there was a variety of colors, many specific colors and color groups were missing. There were very few really bright or dark colors. There was no olive green, fuchsia, or pale yellow. Blues, gray-blues, peaches, pale greens, and reds made up the majority of the colors.

Surrounded by colored supplies, I realized that anyone could walk into that store at any time and buy specific colored supplies related to most art and craft projects. That person could select an exact Pantone color, a specific color of embroidery floss or pencil, or even have paint mixed to exactness. But quilters have always been at the mercy of the fabric designers, fabric manufacturers, and quilt shop owners as to the colors of fabrics available at any one time. Furthermore, fashion trends tend to dictate the colors used in printed cloth and many times certain colors just are not available. Staring at the color products in that store I realized that quilters should have a range of specific colored prints always available to work with, just as other artists and crafts people have standard colors always available to them.

RJR Fashion Fabrics agreed to work with me to develop a collection of fabrics that spanned the color spectrum and would function as a palette for quilters. The fabric collection, which I will refer to as my PALETTE in this book, initially began as 100 colors and was later expanded to 124. The idea was that if quilters could not find a particular color from their own collections or from other manufacturers, they would know that these "standard" colors of printed fabrics would be available to them just as Pantone colors are available to artists and printers. I want to emphasize that in no way can this particular set of fabrics cover every possible color. There are lighter, grayer, darker, clearer, cleaner colors in every area. But my PALETTE covers the general color range and other colors can be added to and shaded with them. Quilters can use the PALETTE colors to fill in and coordinate with other fabrics when certain colors are not generally available. Paper swatches in colors from the PALETTE have been reproduced in the back of this book for your reference, for your use in creating your own master palette, and for doing the exercises. The name I have given to each color is printed on the back of the swatch.

The Three Key Ingredients

Before creating your own master palette, you need to understand the three ingredients that I believe are most important for a successful color scheme.

• SHADING • The first ingredient is *shading*, and the shading element is twofold. (1) There should be several shades of the colors used in a project. For example, a blue color scheme should not contain fabrics that are all the same Williamsburg blue color. Including many shades of blue from lightest to darkest will be more dynamic. If red is added to those blues, you should have several shades of blue *and* several shades of red, shading from pale rose through red into burgundy. (2) Those colors chosen should also shade together. This is the key to my entire system. For instance purple tones might be used to shade the blue and red colors together, turquoise might link blue and green and so on. It is the colors that are used to link the color groups (I call them "transition" colors) that add a unique dimension to the color combination.

• THE DEEP DARK • The second ingredient is a very dark fabric. I call it the *deep dark*. This fabric is a darker version of one of the colors already being used. The deep dark is always relative to the colors it accompanies. In a dark palette, it may be as dark as an intense black, but in a pastel palette it might be a darker version of one of the pastel colors.

• THE ACCENT • The final ingredient is the one I call the *accent*. This is a brighter version of one of the colors already being used. In a blue and green color scheme it might be a brighter green or a brighter blue. The accent is also relative to the other fabrics in the palette. A brighter palette would need a quite bright accent, whereas a less bright accent would work well in a more subtle palette.

These three ingredients work together. Shade *to* your deep dark and accent colors, don't just toss in any dark or bright color unless other shades of that color appear in the palette as well.

Why Make a Master Palette?

It is important for you to create your own master palette by working with the instructions presented here. Why, you may ask, do I need to do that when there are already two of them pictured in this book? The main reason is that you will *learn* from making your palette. You will gain the hands-on experience of seeing how to shade colors together. It's one thing to look at shaded colors and another to actually shade them yourself. Furthermore, you will be forced to work with all colors—those you like and those you may not like. Making a palette will also help you to see the role that the accent and deep dark colors play in the color spectrum, and once you shade 124 colors together, it will be much easier for you to shade fewer colors together when you create individual palettes for various quilting projects.

EXERCISE 1

Creating Your Master Palette

• STEP 1 • *Match the Color Swatches*

Take this book to your fabric collection and match as many colors as possible to the paper swatches on the back pages. It is not necessary to match the print design as well; it is strictly the *color* that you are looking for. Choose prints that are subtle. They should not contain several colors, nor should they be high in contrast. It is difficult to put a fabric with many colors or a bold design into a specific color category since its placement in the palette would depend on which part of the fabric you look at. Those types of fabrics are very important in quilts that use printed fabrics and will be discussed in chapter 3, but for creating the master palette it is best to use prints that almost read as "solids." In fact if you have solid colored fabrics that match any of the paper swatches, use them when prints cannot be found to

match. If your preference is to work only in solid colored fabric, then make the palette entirely from solids.

As you find colors that match, lay the fabric next to the paper swatch in the book and step back several feet to be sure that from a distance they still look the same. If you have been collecting fabrics for many years you probably have quite a few of the colors. If you are lucky you will have them all! In fact, there may be many colors in your fabric collection that are not in the paper swatches. As previously mentioned it is impossible to have all of the colors in the world represented in just 124 fabrics. The ones presented here cover a wide *range* but many other colors could be shaded in with them, and if you have others that will add to the palette, that's great. Just be careful not to let your palette get too cumbersome by trying to work in many more fabrics. What you are looking for is colors that cover the basic spectrum. Then, as you create individual palettes for projects you can incorporate many more shades and prints in your chosen color range.

Suggestion: As a guide for future fabric purchases, cut small pieces from the paper swatches that you were not able to match. Tape those into a purse-sized notebook and keep them handy so that when shopping for fabric you can look for colors to match those you do not have. If you are a new quilter and have a limited collection of fabrics, concentrate future purchases on colors of fabrics that will widen your variety; you will eventually collect a full palette of colors to have at your fingertips.

• STEP 2 • *Cut the Fabric Swatches*

Using the rectangle shown here, make a template from a sturdy plastic or piece of cardboard and cut two swatches from each of the fabrics in the colors you have been able to match. (This rectangle is the same size as the paper swatches in the back of the book.) The purpose of *two* swatches is so that you have one for your master palette and another one to use later for creating individual palettes.

ILLUSTRATION 2 : *Pattern to use for cutting swatches for your palette.*

• STEP 3 • *Find Colors to Fill the Gaps*

If you have managed to find printed or solid colored fabrics to match all of the paper swatches in the back of the book, proceed with the exercise using your own fabric. If you did not find all of the colors, then cut out the paper swatches in the colors you need and use them. If you don't want to cut into the book, look for Pantone colors, swatches of matching colors from magazines, or paint chips in colors to match the missing ones. Or, you may prefer to order a set of fabric swatches. (See Resources section.)

• STEP 4 • *Prepare a Board for Your Palette*

You will need a large piece of heavy white poster board at least 28″ by 22″ (approximately 71cm by 55cm). An even larger one would be better. You can splice two pieces of posterboard together by turning them face down onto a table and pushing the edges next to each other, leaving about a 1/16″ (1.5 mm) gap (do not overlap). Tape the seam with a piece of 2″ (5 cm) wide strapping tape. By leaving a slight gap between the two pieces, the board can later be folded along the seam for easier storage.

Shading the Swatches

The next steps are all based on the principle of shading colors. To create the palette, all of the paper or fabric swatches must be shaded together in a smooth flowing wave of color, where there are no strong contrasts between a light swatch and a dark one and no jumps between one color and another. There are two sample master palettes, both shading all 124 swatches differently, in the back of the book. The best way to learn is by working through the exercise yourself. So, look at the sample palettes only briefly to get an idea of how the colors should flow together and then close those pages and continue the exercise on your own. Later you can compare the palettes in the book with yours, but remember that none of them is "right" or "wrong." In a class of twenty-five students all doing the exercise, no two palettes will be exactly the same.

There are countless possibilities for shading the fabrics. As long as all of the colors flow together smoothly and you cannot tell where one color ends and the other begins, one arrangement is as good as the next.

• STEP 5 • *Sort the Swatches into Groups*

It can be overwhelming at first to be faced with 124 different colors and not know where to begin. The best way to start is by sorting the swatches first into color groups. For instance put all the reds in one pile, the blues in another and so forth. After sorting more or less into color groups, next sort within the groups, separating the clearer tones from the grayer ones. Trying to shade grayed and clear tones together alternately can create a choppy effect. For example, look at the group of clear greens and grayed teals in illustrations 3A and 3B. In the first example, illustration 3A, the colors have been shaded from light to dark, all in one group,

ILLUSTRATION 3A: *Shading all of the greens together can create a choppy effect.*

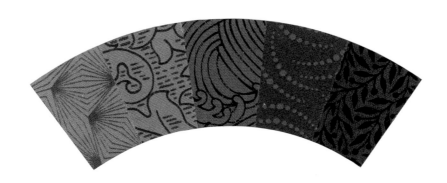

ILLUSTRATION 3B : *Separate the clear tones from the gray tones and shade them separately.*

and in illustration 3B they have been separated into two groups—the grayed teal greens in one and the clearer greens in another. Creating two separate groups of green swatches gives a smoother blending and looks less jumpy and more appealing than trying to shade them all together. It is even possible that the two green groups might appear in totally different places on the master palette, as is the case in the sample master palettes.

• **S T E P 6** • *Shade the Swatches Within Color Groups*

Once the groups have been sorted by color and then by tones, shade within the groups from light to dark. There should be no strong contrasts between a light and a dark color. For instance, navy blue would not go next to pastel blue. Several shades of blue would have to go between them in order to make the transition from the dark to the light.

• **S T E P 7** • *Link the Color Groups Together*

Next link the groups together. Bear in mind that there are many ways to shade from one color to the next, and no one way is necessarily better than another. You could go either through the dark colors or through the light ones. In some cases you may shade from the brightest of one color to the brightest of another, or through medium tones. For instance, to get from red to yellow you might go darker and darker with the reds until they shade to burgundy and then to brown, then to lighter browns and golds and finally to yellow (see illustration 4A). But there are many other ways red and yellow could be shaded together. Three other possibilities are shown in illustrations 4B, 4C, and 4D. Illustration 4B for example shades through light colors, 4C through brights (bright red next to orange and gold), and 4D through less bright, medium tones (red to rust to gold.)

In illustrations 5 and 6, several different ways are

ILLUSTRATION 4A, B : *Two ways to shade from bright red into yellow.*

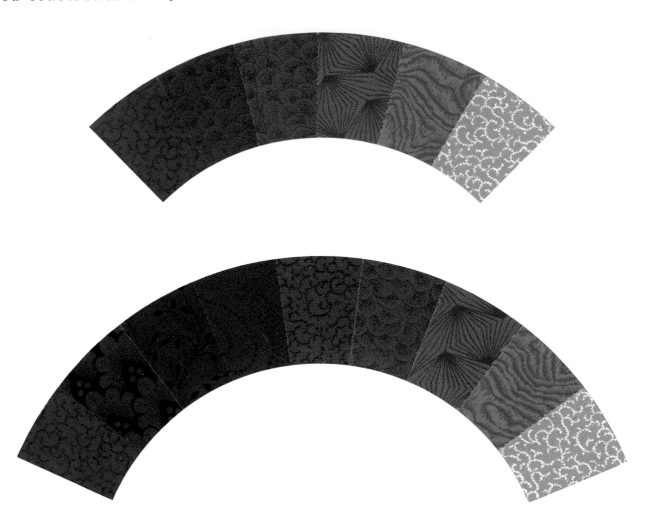

ILLUSTRATION 4C, D : *Two ways to shade from
bright red to yellow.*

shown to shade medium blue to bright green and rose to blue.

Another way to shade two colors together is to add an intermediate color. This can also add depth and interest. For example look again at the four yellow and red shadings in illustrations 4A, B, C, and D and then at the two shadings in illustration 7. The first one includes olive green in the shading between the two colors and the other uses grays and purples.

• **STEP 8** • *Work Through Possible Problems*
Working on the posterboard, place the swatches next to each other, side by side or slightly overlapped. Shade them all together, eventually forming a complete circle. Bear in mind that sometimes no matter how hard you try, you will end up with two ends that won't shade together. Rather than close the circle, resulting in a strong contrast between a value or color, leave the circle open and create an inverted U-shape.

ILLUSTRATION 5 : *Four ways to shade from
medium blue to bright green.*

ILLUSTRATION 6 : *Three ways to shade from rose to blue.*

ILLUSTRATION 7 : *Shading red and yellow with
an intermediate color.*

Often when students are doing this exercise, one or two swatches just don't fit. And it seems like they are never the same swatches. So much depends on how the other colors have been shaded together. If you find a few "odd" pieces, set them aside. Leaving a couple of swatches out is all right, but avoid leaving out a whole group of similar colors.

You also may find that you would like to use the same color more than once, that it could be used in totally different parts of the palette in order to shade certain colors together. If that happens, cut the swatch in half lengthwise and use it in both places. (If it is one of your own fabrics instead of a paper swatch, simply cut another piece.)

• STEP 9 • *Check the Shading*

When all of the swatches are shaded together into a circle or inverted U-shape, run your eye around the swatches slowly several times. Keep asking yourself if there are any strong contrasts between a light swatch and a dark one, or if there are any places where colors do not shade well together. When you are satisfied, tape or glue the swatches to the piece of posterboard.

• STEP 10 • *Add Fabrics from Your Collection*

If you used the paper swatches from the back of the book to make your master palette, go now to the fabric swatches that you cut from your own collection. Place the corresponding fabric partially on top of its matching paper swatch, and tape or glue these in place. You can fill in more swatches as you collect new fabrics. When these are all laid out, it will be immediately apparent which color families you are and are not drawn to. You will most likely have many more swatches in colors you like than in those you do not like; we all have specific preferences and tend to purchase fabrics accordingly. It is not imperative to actually *have* fabrics from all of the colors on the palette. You may never want to make a quilt that contains bright orange or avocado. But it will become apparent, as you read on and experiment, that a basic collection of fabric that encompasses the majority of colors in the spectrum is as valuable to a quilter as a full-color palette of paints is to a painter. Sometimes it is hard to realize that a color considered "ugly" may be just the one that takes a palette combination from ordinary to dynamic. So often I have heard the comment "I never would have thought to use that color; it's one I would never buy, but it makes the quilt!" Remember, it is not the basic colors that you selected for a color scheme that make it work, but what you choose to go with them!

2 EXPERIMENTING WITH COLOR COMBINATIONS FROM THE MASTER PALETTE

Creating the master palette has given you the experience of seeing how to shade colors together and how to work with all colors—those you like and those you may not like. It has also helped to show how the three ingredients of any color scheme—shading, deep dark, and accent—work.

By shading the colors together in the creation of the master palette, you have created scores of different dynamic color combinations simply by using swatches adjacent to each other on the palette. As you'll see in the following exercise, in each of those combinations, no matter where you look on the palette, there are always several shades of each color, as well as the deep dark and the accent.

EXERCISE 2

Consider the Possibilities

Take two lightweight pieces of cardboard such as 3″ by 5″ (7.6cm by 12.7cm) index cards and turn to one of the sample master palettes in this book. Put one of the cards along the side of one of the swatches. Count twenty swatches and put the other card beside the twentieth swatch. Look at the swatches in between and see what an exciting color scheme there is. Move the cards around the chart three or four swatches at a time, each time leaving twenty swatches between the cards. No matter where on the palette you are, there will be a pleasing combination of colors.

Twenty swatches is an arbitrary number. Sometimes additional swatches will enhance the colors even more; sometimes fewer than twenty can look pleasing. The two sample master palette layouts in this book are each shaded differently. If you do the same experiment with both, you will see countless possible color combinations as you move the cards two or three swatches at a time, leaving approximately twenty swatches visible in between. Now do the same experiment with your own palette. See how many truly beautiful color combinations you have created. Whether looking at a light section of the remaining palette or a dark one, there will always be the shading between colors, the deep dark, and the accent. Furthermore, it is likely that some of the most dramatic combinations contain colors you might never have thought to use.

It's All Relative

As you move the cards around the master palette, note the relativity of the deep dark and the accent. In a light section of the palette, the deep dark is relative to those colors next to it—it is always a darker version of one of the other colors but not necessarily very dark. In a pastel or light color grouping, black could be too strong and jarring. On the other hand, in a darker section of the palette, a strong black may be the only color that gives the necessary depth.

The accent works similarly. When looking at a section of the palette that has more subdued, grayer colors, the accent is not as bright as it is in a section where all of the colors are generally brighter. Then it is necessary to go very bright to get the spark.

Some quilters are now working in extremely bright colors. What they are finding is that, because all of the colors are generally so bright, it is necessary to add a touch of an iridescent or metalic fabric to get the intensity needed for the accent.

Does all this mean you can only use colors that are adjacent to each other on one of the master palettes? Not at all. You can use *any* colors! Everyone's palette is unique. The two shown in this book look quite different from each other and I'm sure yours does as well. In each case, different color groups have been linked together, but as long as they have been shaded effec-

tively, they all look good. Likewise, you can choose whatever color groups you want for a project; add whatever other colors you need to shade them together, and you will have a great combination.

The Importance of Shading

The most significant lesson I learned after developing exercises for my color system was the importance of *shading* colors together. I used to tell students that whatever fabrics they chose for a quilt, they also needed several shades of each color plus some type of transition to link the color groups together. What I didn't realize until later, after my system became more fully evolved, was that all of the chosen colors should be shaded together as well! Don't stop with a single transition. For this color system it is important to select all of the colors necessary to shade the fabrics from one color group to the next. The "transition color" only begins the blending process. When all of the colors are shaded together you are forced to add more colors that you might have never thought of using—ones that take the palette from ordinary to exciting. As I mentioned earlier, a deep dark and an accent were two elements that I always felt were important in selecting a palette for a quilt. In shading the groups together, the deep dark and the accent are added automatically. It works every time!

Background Colors

Many quilts have an overall color feeling with subtle contrasts. This is usually the case with one-patch quilts such as the *Tumbling Blocks* quilt on page 109 and "fragmented" quilts, such as the ones on pages 121, 122, and 127. But many other quilts require some fairly strong contrasts in order for the design to show up against the background.

For years the common background for quilts was white or muslin. Then as quilters began using more prints they looked for subtle beige prints to use as backgrounds. But sometimes a color other than beige or white makes a better background. By shading the colors in a palette as explained here, you can continue the shading to the lightest of one of the colors and this can be the backgound even if only a few colors are to be used. Why throw in beige when there are no beige or brown tones in the palette? A pale gray, taupe, lavender or some other color might look far better. See the quilts on pages 44, 65, and 97 and their related palettes for an illustration of this point. No matter how many colors you are planning to use, if all of the colors are first shaded together, the individual ones you end up with, including the background, will harmonize.

Shading Two Colors

The following are several examples of shaded color groups showing how the system works. After reviewing these examples, experiment with several more combinations on your own. The only way to really feel comfortable with this theory is to work with it yourself.

Example: Yellow and Purple. Look at master palette 2 in the back of the book. To shade yellow into purple it would not be necessary to incorporate all the colors on the palette between purple and yellow (coral, rust, burgundy, olive, tan, pink, and red).

Look at illustration 8. Obviously, the group of yellows does not shade smoothly into the purples. What is needed for them to shade together?

One possibility would be to go from yellow through gold into browns to very dark brown, black, and then to the dark purples and on to the lighter purples. That's exactly what I did in illustration 9.

ILLUSTRATION 8: *Groups of yellows and purples that are not shaded together.*

ILLUSTRATION 9 : *Yellows and purples shaded through browns and flowing into a touch of red.*

When selecting swatches from a master palette, I always go a little farther with one of the colors to subtly shade into a new color because this sometimes adds interest. In this case, the purple swatches shaded into red, so I added four red swatches. Cover the four red swatches with a piece of paper. Do you like the arrangement better with or without the red?

It is also possible to shade from the pale yellows to beige and then into a hint of just about any other pale color.

See what happens when the light end is shaded into a touch of turquoise (illustration 10). This raises the problem of what I call an either/or situation. In my opinion the addition of both the red swatches at one end and the turquoise on the other is too much. There is one too many colors. But it is a matter of personal preference as to which one to use. Cover the four red swatches, but leave the turquoise. Next cover the turquoise swatches, leaving the red. Which do you prefer?

One exciting factor about this whole system is that there are so many ways to shade any two colors together, and all of them will look good as long as you *do* shade them. Just choose the arrangement you like the best. For instance in the previous example, you may like the purple and yellows but do not want to use any brown fabrics. Then try shading another way. Link purple and yellow together through the light colors

ILLUSTRATION 10: *The yellows and purples shading into hints of both turquoise and red.*

ILLUSTRATION 11: *Yellow and purple linked through gray.*

rather than through the dark. The next example (illustration 11) goes lighter with the purple tones, through gray and very pale gray and then into the yellow. The addition of gray is something you might never have thought of, but it forms the link. Gray is not the most attractive color in the world by itself, but it is the type of color that shading forces us to use, and that makes the color scheme work!

While the shading of the above example is all right, I feel it needs some additional colors. Look what happens when the yellows continue through gold again

(illustration 12), but this time instead of shading into brown tones, they shade into olive green.

What if you don't like the gold and olive and want to stay with just the pale yellows and not use the more brassy yellow? Add another color by shading from the dark end. Look on your master palette and select any swatches that shade into very dark. There are many possibilities. In the examples in illustration 13A and 13B, one is shaded into turquoise and the other into fuchsia.

ILLUSTRATION 12 : *Yellow and purple linked through gray and shading from the yellows to olive green.*

ILLUSTRATION 13A : *Shading from the
purple end into turquoise.*

ILLUSTRATION 13B : *Shading from the purple end into fuchsia.*

How Does Taste Fit In?

At this point I want to make a small digression. For years students would come to me and say "You never use yellow in your quilts. Don't you like yellow? Is yellow not a good color?" It was true: my quilts didn't have yellow in them. I never knew exactly why I didn't like using yellow, it just never seemed to work for me. But I was always careful not to discourage anyone else from using that color. Yellow was specifically used in the previous example for the benefit of those people who asked about yellow all those years.

Once I developed my color system and the concept of a master palette for quilters, I realized *why* yellow always eluded me. There were rarely any yellow fabrics on the market, and if there were, they were always the same brassy yellow. There never seemed to be any variation in color—any shading from pale to darker yellow or any way to get from darker yellow to another color. The reason I had never used yellow in my quilts, even though I hadn't realized it, was that there was not enough variety of yellow fabrics to give the shading necessary to allow it to flow into another color. It was always a color thrown in that didn't relate well to the others because it stood alone.

All quilters like some colors better than others and tend to buy more fabrics in their favorite colors. I am no different. When I began designing my PALETTE fabric collection, I first sat down with swatches of all the fabrics I had previously designed, then separated them by color. Finally I tried to shade them all together as in one of the master palettes. I was astonished to find there were some colors that I had never used in a fabric design, and there were others that I had repeated numerous times. Many of the new colors I had to make for the PALETTE were ones I don't particularly like. Just as many people only purchase fabric in their favorite colors, I was also *designing* fabrics in my taste of colors! Interestingly enough, of the new fabrics in the PALETTE, four of them were yellow. Obviously I had even shied away from designing yellow, but my discovery was, that if there are several shades of yellow, and they can be shaded together with the other colors, then yellow can work.

I must say, as a fabric designer it is very difficult to get a good yellow. If yellow and white are put together the contrast is so small that it is difficult to see the design. As soon as another color is added to the yellow, no matter how pale the yellow is, the color changes. Suffice it to say that if you find any good yellow fabrics, it would be advisable to buy at least small pieces of them. They are few and far between.

Shading Pale Colors Together

One of the most popular color combinations students bring to class is peach and green. Those wanting to use a peach and green color combination will

ILLUSTRATION 14 : *Peaches and greens* not *shaded together.*

invariably bring a few pale peach colored fabrics and a few pale green colored fabrics. While both of these colors are very nice, I find the combination of them alone is boring. The problem is that there is no variety in shades of color, no deep dark, and no accent.

Selecting peach and green is a good start, but shading those colors together will make a much more exciting combination. "But how can I shade from peach to green?" a student will ask. It seems impossible at first to get from one of those colors to the other. However, peach and green can be shaded together in many different ways; none is necessarily better than another. For instance in illustration 15, the two colors have been shaded through dark tones. Peach has gone from rust to brick red, red, burgundy, eggplant, black, and then through the dark greens and brighter greens until it flows to the original pale greens.

In illustration 16, instead of the peaches shading into

ILLUSTRATION 15 : *Peaches and greens shaded through dark tones (rusts and reds).*

rusts and reds, they have been shaded into pinks and fuchsias, and instead of shading through the brighter green to the gray-greens, the shading has gone through the teals. Two additional combinations (not shown here) could be made by shading the peaches and rusts into the teals or by shading the peaches and fuchsias into the brighter greens. It is a matter of personal preference as to which one is better.

However, you might say upon seeing these combinations, that those palettes are too dark for you, that

ILLUSTRATION 16 : *Peaches and greens shaded through dark tones (teals and fuchsias).*

you wanted a more pastel look to your quilt. As I show in illustration 17, you could shade through the lights, instead of the darks, going lighter still with the peach and green until they can blend together. But don't forget the deep dark. Shade a little darker with each of the two colors until you achieve enough depth of color for the deep dark. Instead of black as in the previous combinations, you would use darker shades of green and peach or red. Remember also that the *amount* of dark and light colored fabrics you use in a quilt will affect its overall appearance. This is discussed later in the chapter; see Proportion of Color and Value.

Try this experiment with illustration 17: Cover the three red swatches on the far right and the three green ones on the far left. Do you see what happens to the colors without the deep dark? Try it with only the reds covered or with only the greens. Both are needed.

While the combination in illustration 17 is nice, it is not dynamic. What it really needs is another color. But you can't just throw any old color in. The new color must also be shaded. You could shade from the greens into blue without going any darker, but it would still give a darker appearance to the palette because the blue would be medium in tone. The same would occur

ILLUSTRATION 17 : *Peaches and greens shaded through light tones.*

ILLUSTRATION 18 : *Peaches and greens shaded through light tones with a hint of yellow.*

if you tried shading into another color from the red. If you desire to maintain a pastel look, the best way to go would be through the lights. Look what happens when a hint of yellow is added (illustration 18).

In this case, the yellow has added a new dimension (I can't believe this is me saying that!), but at the same time I think now that the yellow has been added, perhaps something has to come off either end. Cover over the last red swatch and see if it looks better. Then try covering over the last green swatch. With the addition of the yellow, one or the other should be eliminated, but not both. If you eliminate both sides the deep dark is lost and the colors go flat.

Working with Loose Swatches

The master palette is a great reference, but it is also useful to have loose fabric or paper swatches for experimenting with. If you do not have a set of fabric swatches, cut about one third off of the paper swatches that you have arranged on the posterboard. This will provide a set of loose swatches for the following exercises and for experimenting with on your own. For the time being lay them on the posterboard in the same layout as the master palette. Later, when you're not using them, you can store them in a small plastic bag or envelope.

EXERCISE 3

Shading Two Colors Together

Using the paper swatches that you cut from your palette or your own fabrics (if you have matched all of the colors), see how many different ways you can shade together the colors shown in illustration 19. (The color names refer to the names printed on the back of each paper swatch; these coincide with the names of the colors in my fabric PALETTE.)

Begin by looking at your master palette and the two samples in this book. See where each of the colors falls on the various palettes. Take those colors from the loose swatches. Make sure to take whole groups of colors, not just individual ones so that there are several shades of each color. Lay those groups in front of you and rearrange them to shade the groups together.

First take each swatch and all of the fabrics next to it, going to the *darkest* point, and see if the darks on each set will shade together. Next, do the same thing, but this time going to the *lightest* swatch and see if the lights shade together. Try shading them through medium values or through brights, or even with another color in between. Most likely additional swatches will have to be added to get the necessary shading; you might need to pick individual colors from here and there on the palette to shade all of them together.

Experiment with shading each of these in at least four different ways. You will be amazed at how much better the two colors look when they are shaded together.

1. Ocher and Cobalt

2. Terra Cotta and Fuchsia

3. Apple Green and Burnt Orange

4. Wedgewood and Poppy

5. Holiday Green and Fuchsia

6. Carnation and Olive

ILLUSTRATION 19 : *Experiment with shading each of these two-color groups.*

Shading More Than Two Colors Together

Until now we have been taking only two colors and shading them together and then sometimes shading beyond one of the colors to get a touch of another. What if you start out with more than one color to begin with? Would you think I had gone crazy if I said I was going to make a quilt with hot pink, bright olive, orange, and purple?

ILLUSTRATION 20: *What would you think about the possibility of shading hot pink, olive, orange, and purple?*

ILLUSTRATION 21: *Hot pink, olive, orange, and purple shaded together.*

These colors (illustration 20) look quite garish by themselves, but look what happens in illustration 21 when they are all shaded together. The addition of muddy brown, khaki, peach, and grayed lavender as well as all the shades of the various colors, give what was needed to link all of those colors together. In fact that is the palette I chose for my quilt, *Sundance*, shown on page 62.

shown on page 62.

EXERCISE 4

Shading Three or More Colors Together

If you have managed to shade each of the color pairs together you are now ready to shade three colors. In illustration 22 there are some three-color sets for you to play with. One way to begin is to select a color from the three in the group that you would like to be most prominent. Then shade that color to the darkest on one side of it and the lightest on the other. Then link one of the other colors through the lights and the other through the darks. It is also possible that two of the colors could be linked through bright or medium tones rather than light or dark. It might be necessary to add another color in order to link them all together. Once you shade these, select three or more colors of your own and do the same exercise.

  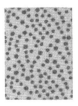

1. Toffee, Wedgewood, and Celadon

2. Peach, Scarlet, and Periwinkle

3. Carnation, Jade, and Olive

4. Ash, Scarlet, and Carnation

ILLUSTRATION 22 : *Shade each of these three-color groups together.*

Monochromatic Quilt Color Schemes

You may prefer a monochromatic color scheme—all blues, all black and gray, all red, and so on—rather than one with many colors. While a quilt made in only one color can be very effective, I think it can be even more dramatic if the color shades into a hint of another color.

For example, a gray and black palette is shown in illustration 23. While a quilt done with those colors could be quite handsome, a touch of another color shaded to either the dark end or the light end can provide additional interest without taking away the initial impact of a gray and black quilt. Shading could come from the black side of the palette into almost any other dark color—purple, burgundy, olive green, navy, teal, and so on. Likewise, the shading could come from the other end into a touch of pale yellow, pink, or green. See the examples in illustration 24. In each case, the impact is still that of a monochromatic gray and black palette, but the addition of a touch of another color has added interest to the palette.

ILLUSTRATION 23 : *Palette made of only gray and black.*

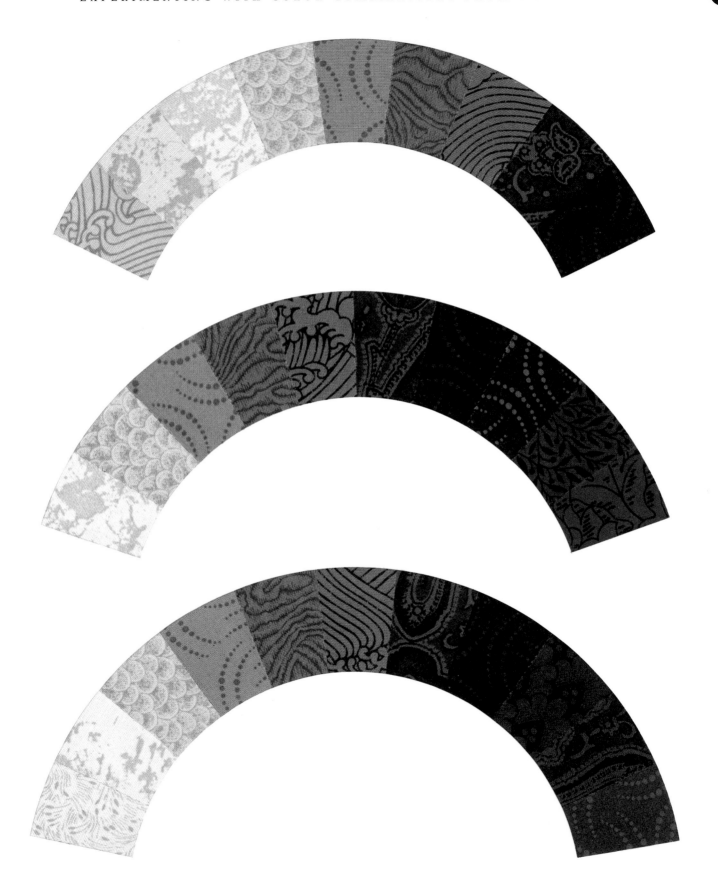

ILLUSTRATION 24 : *Gray and black palettes including hints of another color.*

ILLUSTRATION 25 : Stars over the Mountain *by Kay Lettau.*

Look at Kay Lettau's quilt *Stars over the Mountain*. The initial color impact is that it is made of blacks and grays, but closer study shows hints of other colors. She predominantly used gray and black fabrics, but her palette shaded into beige on one end and rust/browns on the other. Blue/gray colored fabrics shaded through the grays. Her palette is shown in illustration 26.

ILLUSTRATION 26 : *Palette of colors Kay Lettau used to make her quilt* Stars over the Mountain.

Now look at the two *Boxes and Stars* quilts shown in illustrations 27 and 29. Which one do you prefer? The first one is made up of a palette of strictly blue colored fabrics. The second one has hints of lavender shaded into the light end and deep purple at the dark end and even some periwinkle blue shaded with the medium blue colors. However, the immediate reaction to that quilt would still be that it is a monochromatic blue quilt.

ILLUSTRATION 27 : Boxes and Stars *in blues, designed and pieced by Jinny Beyer.*

ILLUSTRATION 28 : *Palette used for quilt in illustration 27.*

ILLUSTRATION 29 : Boxes and Stars *in blues with hints of lavender, designed by Jinny Beyer*

ILLUSTRATION 30 : *Palette used for quilt in illustration 29.*

Working with a Monochromatic Color Scheme

Here's another experiment. Turn to one of the two master palettes in this book or to your own. Select a group of swatches that fall into a color family, such as blues, reds, greens, or yellows. Put a piece of paper or index card on either side of the group and then move one of the cards one swatch at a time until there is a subtle shading into another color. Do the same thing with the other side of the color group. Continue around the palette with all of the colors. With a limited number of swatches you can achieve a monochromatic color scheme, but the subtle hint of another color will add more life.

Proportion of Color and Value

A palette is just that—a palette of colors. How you use the palette can make a huge difference in the overall effect of the quilt. The important thing to remember is that the palette is a guide. It tells you which colors are going to look good together and which ones need to be included in order to have a harmonious color effect. The manner in which that palette is interpreted depends on the proportions of each color used, how bright, how dark, how light, how dull, how bold the individual quiltmaker wants that quilt to be.

Don't make the mistake of looking at a palette you have created and saying that it is no good because it is

ILLUSTRATION 31: *Palette used for Kay Sorensen's quilts,* Color Study 1, Color Study 2, *and* Color Study 3.

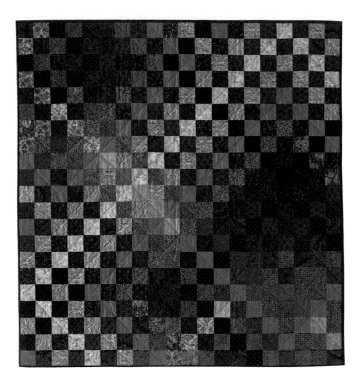

ILLUSTRATION 32 : Color Study 1, *made by Kay Sorensen.*

ILLUSTRATION 33 : Color Study 2, *made by Kay Sorensen.*

too dark. Remember that, in the palette, you are looking at equal amounts of each individual color. If you don't want the quilt to be so dark, use very small portions of the darks and more of the lights when making the quilt.

Kay Sorensen did an interesting study of color in a series of quilts she made. She began with the basic palette shown in illustration 31 and chose to use a simple two inch square (5.1 cm) not including the seam allowance. Working with varying amounts of the colors, lights, and darks in the palette she created the first three quilts in the series.

Color Study 1 is much lighter than the other two because it uses many more light squares than the others. *Color Study 2* is not only the darkest, but it is also the boldest, mainly because of the concentration of the brightest colors (orange and red) and the sharp contrast between them and the dark black. Interestingly enough, *Color Study 1* has many more orange and red squares than *Color Study 2*, but the boldness has been diffused because of the lack of strong contrast between those colors and some of those adjacent to them. Furthermore, there are the *same* number of orange and red squares in *Color Study 2* as in *Color Study 3*. Once again in *Color Study 3* the orange and red do not appear so bold as in *Color Study 2* because they do not fall next to the dark black.

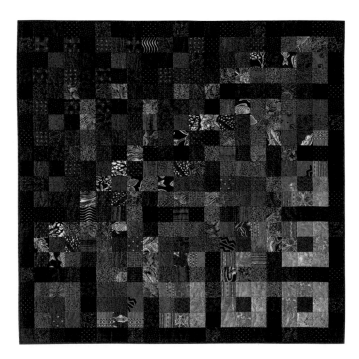

ILLUSTRATION 34 : Color Study 3, *made by Kay Sorensen.*

ILLUSTRATION 35 : *Expanded palette with the addition of gold and yellow,
used by Kay Sorensen to make the quilts in illustrations 36, 37, and 38.*

ILLUSTRATION 36 : *Charm quilt* Color Study 4,
made by Kay Sorensen.

ILLUSTRATION 37 : Color Study 5, *made by Kay Sorensen.*

Kay next wanted to make a charm quilt (a quilt where every piece is cut from a *different* fabric), and in order to have more choice in the fabrics available to her she decided to expand the palette. She shaded from the olive greens into mustard, gold, and yellow (illustration 35). *Color Study 4* is lighter than the previous three, but it is strictly a matter of the *proportions* of the light and dark fabrics she chose to use.

Color Study 5 and *Color Study 6* use the same expanded palette as the charm quilt (*Color Study 4*). In both of these quilts the gold and yellow are much more prominent than in the charm quilt. *Color Study 5* is much bolder and darker than *Color Study 6*, which has a more delicate appearance in the colors being used. But of greatest interest is that these two quilts not only were made from the same palette, but they also contain exactly the same fabrics. The *only* difference between the two is that in *Color Study 5*, the light starts in the center of the quilt and goes to the dark on the outside and *Color Study 6* is exactly reversed. Because of this, the proportion of light and dark is reversed. But the order of which fabric is next to which is exactly the same.

The example of these two quilts graphically illustrates how the proportion of light, dark, and color can

ILLUSTRATION 38 : Color Study 6, *made by Kay Sorensen.*

completely influence the final project. A person looking at the palette used in the last three quilts might say that it is too dark, that black is too oppressive to use in a quilt. But cover over the black swatches on the palette (illustration 35) and see what happens when the black is eliminated. *Color Study 6* contains only one completely black square, which is in the very center of the quilt. Look also at what happens when that black

center is eliminated (illustration 39). The deep dark is gone and something now seems lacking in the colors. The black *is* important to the palette, but if a light effect is desired, then that color only needs to be used in small portions.

You'll be applying these principles of proportion of color and value in chapter 6, Palette Practice with Quilts.

ILLUSTRATION 39 : *Kay Sorensen's* Color Study 6 *quilt with center black square eliminated. Compare this with illustration 38.*

Chapter **3** USING PRINTS FOR VISUAL TEXTURE

The master palettes shown in chapter 1 and the ones you have created are strictly palettes of *colors*. I would never make a quilt using only the fabrics I designed for my PALETTE, nor would you want to make one using only the fabrics in your master palette. The fabrics chosen for the various palettes are of necessity subtle, non-contrasting prints chosen in order to blend and coordinate with other prints. They are the base on which to build exciting color and fabric schemes for any quilting project. But if your choice is to work in prints and not solid colored fabrics, color is only one of the ingredients of your quilt. The type of prints you choose also plays a very important role in the outcome of the project.

A Variety of Prints

Multi-colored prints, medium to large scale prints, and prints with a variety of design motifs need to be added to supplement the palette of colors. These will give the quilt variety and contrast and make it come alive with "texture" as well as color. This texture is a *visual* one, not a tactile one. We are used to thinking of texture in fabric as the difference between seersucker, silk, taffeta, and so forth. But the *visual* texture—what the eye sees on the surface of the quilt, and the way the prints play against each other—is a very important ingredient in the overall planning of a quilt. The only way to achieve that visual texture is to have a wide variety in the *type* of prints being used and also in the

ILLUSTRATION 40 : *A nice balance of colors, but the textures are too similar. The black and white version more easily shows the similarity of the prints.*

scale of those prints. When good visual texture is achieved a viewer is apt to want to touch the quilt—to try feeling what he or she sees. Some quilts look like they have been made of silk even when they contain only 100 percent cotton fabrics. Other quilts have a surface that appears far from smooth. The combination of prints gives the illusion.

There are many types of prints, and you will want to train your eye to see those differences. Look for hard lines—checks, weaves, stripes, angles—and soft lines—curves, swirls, flowers, leaves. Some prints are more solid in appearance, some are mottled, some have high contrasts, and so on.

Seeing in Black and White

When I am designing fabrics for a new collection or selecting fabrics for a quilt I often photocopy the prints. I find it so much easier to see visual texture differences when I am not also being influenced by the color. You may also find it beneficial to look at prints initially in black and white. Notice the example of colors in illustration 40. The balance of the colors looks good, but the textures are much too similar. A black and white rendition of the fabrics emphasizes the similarity of the prints.

Look how much more interesting those same colors are when a variety of textures is used. In the examples in illustration 41, both the color and black and white versions have much more textural interest.

Just as *I* like to work first in black and white, I also have my *students* work with visual texture by first

ILLUSTRATION 41: *The same colors as illustration 40, but more variety in the textures. Once again the black and white illustrates the differences.*

studying photocopies of different types of prints. Color can greatly influence the way someone perceives a fabric, and by eliminating color it becomes easier to see the differences in the prints.

Several types of prints are shown in black and white in illustration 42. I have sorted these prints according to various categories as I perceive them. Prints from small to large scale are included in each group. Mine is certainly not the only way to categorize prints; other people may choose to sort them differently.

EXERCISE 6

How Much Variety in Your Prints?

Often when I am teaching I ask the students to look over the fabrics they have brought. Invariably many of any one person's fabrics are very similar in nature—all small calicos, all checks, all large florals, and so on.

Next I ask how many people in the class have a fabric that does not contain a leaf or a flower. I will hear a chuckle, a gasp, an "Oh my goodness," as they realize almost all of their fabrics contain flowers and leaves. Check your own fabrics and see if this is not the case. It isn't really your fault. At least 85 percent of the printed fabrics in most quilt shops contain leaves or flowers, and at least 90 percent have leaves, flowers, or some type of curve. I try to keep this in mind as I design fabrics and use many different types of designs for my prints.

This is not to say that you should refrain from buying fabric that has flowers or leaves. Rather, be aware that a variety of fabric motifs can add a new dimension to your quilts. Study the types of prints shown in illustration 42, and then check your fabrics and see how much variety you have in the types of prints you have purchased. Are there some categories where you have an

PAISLEY

LEAVES

REPRESENTATIONAL

DOTS

WEAVES AND PLAIDS

ILLUSTRATION 42 : *Black and white renditions of fabrics showing a variety of textural differences.*

GEOMETRICS

FLORAL

LINEAR

VINES

SWIRL

abundance of prints and others where you have none? How many totally different types of textures appear in the printed fabrics you have purchased? We are often more attracted by the color of a piece of fabric than we are by the print, and an inventory of your fabric collection may show a great similarity in the types of prints, even though there is a much larger variety in the colors. If a survey of your fabric collection shows that the majority of the prints are of a certain type of design, then specifically seek out those prints that are different from the ones you already have.

Don't be fooled by the size of a print. While a small print fabric with a vine on it will look quite different from a larger print with a vine, the patterns will be similar; better to try to find other motifs. In illustration 43, the top portion shows several sizes of prints, but all with vine motifs. If you are using only a few fabrics in a quilt, one fabric with a vine on it should suffice. It would be more interesting for the motifs on the other fabrics to be completely different, with a good variety in visual textures, as are the fabrics in the bottom portion of the illustration. Cover over the bottom swatches and look only at those on top. Next cover over the top swatches. Which do you prefer?

ILLUSTRATION 43: *The top of the illustration shows a good combination of colors, but the prints all contain vine motifs. The bottom portion shows the same colors, but with a wider variety of textural differences.*

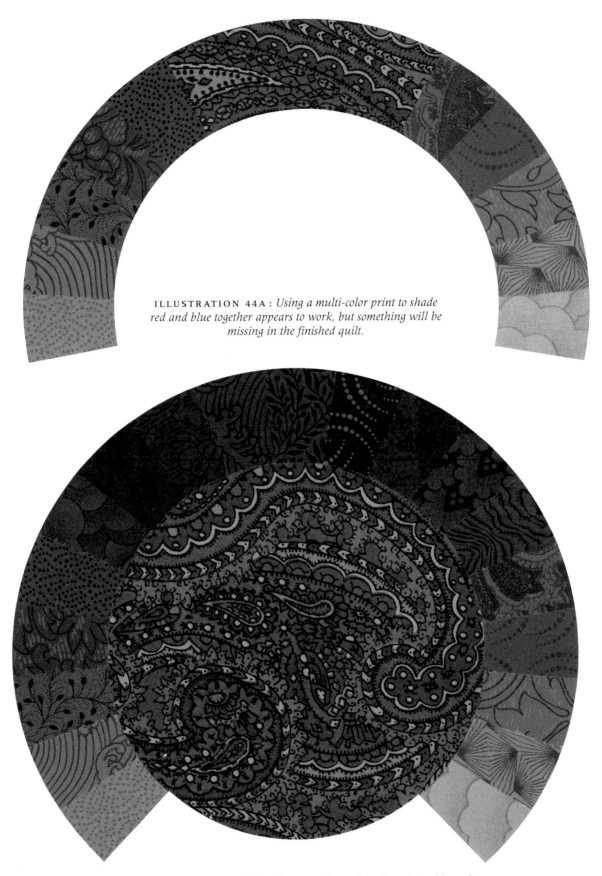

ILLUSTRATION 44A: *Using a multi-color print to shade red and blue together appears to work, but something will be missing in the finished quilt.*

ILLUSTRATION 44B: *This palette puts the multi-color print aside and adds the colors needed to shade red and blue together.*

ILLUSTRATION 45 : *Two sections of* Sundance *quilt where two multi-color prints (green and brown in one and rust and purple in the other) have been used as transitions to shade the colors.*

Avoiding Common Mistakes with Multi-Color Prints

As important as multi-color and different textural prints are in a quilt, do not make the mistake of allowing a multi-color print to act as an element in the color shading of a palette. Often when I am working on color with a group of students, one person will have several shades of two colors, say blue and red, and will link them together, not through shading of darks, lights, or brights, but with a multi-color print which contains both blue and red as in illustration 44A. The person thinks that because the multi-color print has colors from the two groups it can be used to link those groups and will create a shaded palette.

A multi-color print *can* act as a transition between one color and another in your quilt if you are also shading the *other base colors* together. You may even want to use a combination such as the one in 44A in a project where fabrics are shaded together. But as far as the color impact of the entire quilt is concerned, something will be missing unless base colors are also shaded together and at least some of each of those colors are used in the final quilt, as in the illustration 44B. Look at illustration 6 to see some other ways that red and blue can be shaded together.

In the sections of my quilt *Sundance* shown in illustration 45, multi-color prints have been used as transitions—between green and brown in one section and between rust and purple in the other. It is interesting to shade this way in certain parts of the quilt, but compare this section to the entire palette and quilt (illustrations 46 and 47). The quilt would lose impact if colors from the entire palette were not used in various places throughout.

While it is very important for the overall effect to have multi-colored prints of various scales in a quilting project, an attempt should not be made to create the basic palette of colors with those multi-colored prints. So much of the color impact depends on which part of the print is used. When creating a palette, I like to shade the basic colors together and then include the multi-colored prints to one side.

ILLUSTRATION 46 : *Palette of colors used for* Sundance.

ILLUSTRATION 47 : Sundance, *made by Jinny Beyer.*

Chapter **4** USING FEWER FABRICS VERSUS MANY FABRICS

The color system discussed thus far has dealt with the shading of numerous colors together. To make a quilt with *all* of these colors would entail using many different fabrics. Students often ask, "But what if I only want a *few* fabrics in my quilt? I would never be able to use that many fabrics. My pattern has places for only five fabrics."

The Advantages of Using Many Fabrics

First of all I like to explain how much more exciting it can be to work with many fabrics in a quilt. You have seen from the palettes created in the previous chapters how dynamic the colors become when many of them are working together. Of all the quilts I have made, only one of them contains fewer than twenty fabrics. In fact most of them have at least fifty different ones. People often ask me how I achieve the glow that occurs in some of my quilts. It comes from using so many fabrics and being able to shade the brights next to fabrics of similar color with less brightness or intensity. The shading creates a subtle contrast so the vivid prints do not stand out too much.

Many of the colors in my quilt *Sundance* (shown opposite) are quite bright. For example look at the isolated section shown in illustration 48A. The bright oranges and fuchsias, by being clustered and shaded together, do not jump out as much as if the brightest

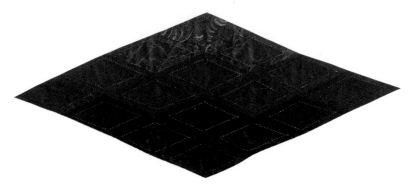

ILLUSTRATION 48A: *Section of* Sundance *containing bright fuchsia, shaded with adjacent colors.*

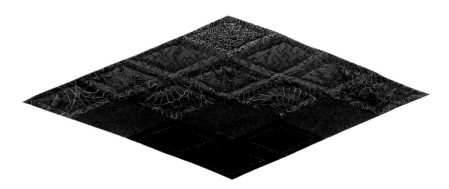

ILLUSTRATION 48B: *Section of* Sundance *containing more subdued colors, with the fuchsia added. Now the fuchsia stands out.*

fuchsia alone were used in a different section. See what happens when we take that fuchsia to a different section of the quilt containing more subtle shades, where it does not blend with the other fabrics (illustration 48B). Now it stands out and is visually very jarring. And yet when that color is subtly shaded with similar types of colors it helps to create a "glow." The bright colors are just as important as the duller ones, and having many different *shades* of the colors makes the difference.

But not every quilt is suited to having shaded sections within the design. Quilts made up of repeat blocks of the same pattern can use only a few different fabrics in each block. However, if each block looks exactly the same, the project may get boring. So, even in this situation it is fun to use several fabrics and to make each block a little different. For continuity you might plan to use navy blue or some other color in a particular place in the block, but you could have different shades or degrees of brightness of that color as well as different textures. The *Rolling Star* quilt shown in illustration 76 contains a number of different fabrics. The stars in each block are always red and navy blue

but not the same red and blue. Sometimes the colors are darker, brighter, or lighter, but red and blue are always used in the same place in each block and within each block they are always the darkest fabrics. Likewise the corner triangles of the blocks are always gold or olive green, but once again many different gold and green fabrics were used. And in the case of all of them, care was taken to find many different types of prints to achieve a good textural balance.

If you don't always want to use the same *color* in a particular place in each block, another possibility is to plan to place different colors of the same *value* in the same position in the blocks. Use a variety of colors from the palette, but have dark, medium, and light colors fall in the same place each time.

Look at Loanne Hamje's quilt (illustration 49) and the palette of colors she chose (illustration 50). No two blocks are the same, yet the quilt has a feeling of unity because she has followed a similar order in the placement of color values within the blocks. Even though different colors have been used, the largest compass points are always the darkest of the fabrics, but in some blocks they are darker or brighter than in others. The

ILLUSTRATION 49: Mariner's Compass *made by Loanne Hamje.*

ILLUSTRATION 50: *Palette used for Loanne Hamje's* Mariner's Compass *quilt.*

next set of points is always medium in value, but that value changes depending on the depth of color of the other fabrics in that particular block. Studying this quilt will help you to see how a palette of many colors can be used effectively.

Paring a Palette of Many Colors Down to a Few

Although effective, a multi-color "scrap" look may not be your style. It may be your desire to use only a few fabrics and have a more ordered appearance to the quilt. Take heart: Quilts made with only six or seven different fabrics can be as beautiful as those made with many.

Even if you want to use only a few fabrics, a fully shaded palette will be an invaluable tool, if you know how to adapt it to your needs. It can be overwhelming to go into a quilt shop with plans to make a new quilt with only a few fabrics and hopes of coming up with the perfect color scheme. With so many bolts of fabrics in a huge array of colors it is difficult to know where to begin. If you have planned a color palette ahead of time, you can go into the shop and immediately zero in on fabrics that match the palette. Instead of choosing among a thousand bolts of fabric in the shop, the scope has been limited to the colors on your particular palette and the task becomes easier.

Even when you want only a few fabrics in a quilt, I recommend starting with a larger palette similar to the ones that we have created so far in the book. Decide which main colors to use and then shade those colors together. This still provides a range of colors to look for while allowing you to eliminate many of the fabrics in the shop. If you have a palette that has been shaded together and contains the three key ingredients—shading colors, the deep dark, and the accent—work with individual colors from the palette and different types of prints in the shop until you find a balance of the few that work well together.

When planning to use fewer than ten different fabrics in a quilt, bear in mind that a variety of visual textures becomes even more important. For instance, if all of the fabrics were small printed calicoes the overall effect could be monotonous. Each print should be different: Aim for at least one large print, and make

sure there are designs with angles as well as curves, hard effects and soft effects. Be aware that it sometimes is difficult to balance both color and print. You may find the perfect colors only to discover that three of the fabrics are the same print! This may or may not be a problem, depending on the total number of fabrics in your quilt. When working with many fabrics in a quilt, having different colored fabrics of the same design is not as big a concern because there will be many more fabrics to balance them out. But when there are only a few fabrics, the visual effect will be much better if the prints are all different. So how do you go about selecting just a few colors? Follow these three steps.

• STEP 1 • *Choose Your Colors and Shade Them Together*

First choose colors you would like to work with. For example, the main colors I wanted to have in my quilt *Borealis* shown in illustration 51 were red and lavender. In order to shade from red to lavender I had to go

ILLUSTRATION 51: Borealis, *made by Jinny Beyer.*

ILLUSTRATION 52: *The red and lavender that were initially chosen for* Borealis *and the palette shading them together.*

from bright red (my accent) to burgundy into purple and then through black (my deep dark), eggplant, fuchsia, and on to lavender. I shaded a little beyond the red into some pink and a little beyond the lavender into periwinkle, pale blue, and gray. As you go through this process, don't worry that you have too large a palette. The shading of all these colors is going to help you determine the essential colors, even if you end up using only a few.

• STEP 2 • *Evaluate and Adjust Your Colors*

After you shade your colors together, see if anything seems to be missing. When the palette for *Borealis* was complete it looked to me like it needed something else. It already had an accent and a deep dark, so maybe it needed another color. I looked on my various master palettes to see what colors the pinks had been shaded into and what colors the grays had gone into. On one of the charts the gray began shading into a pale turquoise. I tried that and it seemed just what I needed. However, any more greens beyond the hint of pale ones were too much. Cover over the three green swatches of the palette in illustration 52 and see the difference they make.

• STEP 3 • *Eliminate Colors*

This was the complete palette I used for *Borealis*. But what if I wanted only eight fabrics in my quilt and didn't want to use all of those colors in between red and lavender? Using the palette as the guide, I eliminated colors as follows and ended up with the pared-down palette in illustration 53A. Since red and lavender were the two original colors, I selected at least two shades of red and two shades of lavender. Because there is a limit on the number of fabrics to be used, those shades had to be different. One fabric had to be one of the "transition" colors that was the link between lavender and red, such as a purple tone. Since the pale turquoise was so essential to the overall palette, I also selected that. The pinks on the other side of the palette helped to make the color scheme complete as well, therefore one of the fabrics needed to be in the pink family. Most likely I would also need a very light color for a background.

When paring down colors, remember to keep the deep dark and the accent—the darker and brighter versions of one or two of the colors. The palette in illustration 53A is composed of eight colors—two shades of red (one of which is the accent), a pink, two shades of lavender, a teal, a gray, and a deep dark purple. See what happens when the deep dark fabric is taken away (illustration 53B) and what happens when the accent is taken away (53C). To get a better visual picture of the three examples, cover all but the one you are looking at with a piece of paper. Also look again at illustration 53A and cover the green swatch. Do you see what happens? That green is as important to the limited palette as it is to the expanded palette.

Tip: When selecting a few colors to use from a larger palette it is tempting to choose the colors you like the best. What you need to remember is that if you prefer a brighter palette, a few of the duller, drabber colors make the bolder, brighter ones even more outstanding. If you prefer a softer, more muted palette, a few brighter colors will enhance it even more. If all of the colors are too similar in nature, then none of them will look as good together.

EXERCISE 7

Selecting Fewer Colors from a Larger Palette

This exercise will provide the chance to practice what you've just learned. Turn to one of the two sample master palettes in this book or the one you have created. Once again select any twenty colors in a row—put pieces of paper or index cards on either side of the twenty to isolate the colors. Keep moving the cards a few swatches at a time until you find a combination you like. Find those same twenty colors in your loose swatches and arrange them in the same order. Now pare those twenty swatches down to six. Find a deep dark, an accent, and a light color for a background and then experiment with adding others until you have a pleasing combination. I recommend you do this exercise several times, until you feel confident about your color choices.

ILLUSTRATION 53A : *Eight colors selected from the expanded palette.*

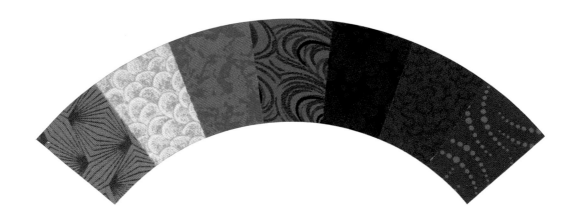

ILLUSTRATION 53B : *The deep dark has been eliminated.*

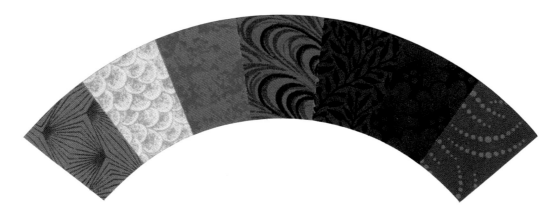

ILLUSTRATION 53C : *The accent has been eliminated.*

Chapter **5** DESIGNING A PALETTE TO COORDINATE WITH A MULTI-COLOR PRINT

A group of shop owners will nod their heads in unison when asked if they have ever had a customer come into their shop hoping to find fabrics for a quilt that will go well with a multi-color fabric or wallpaper—what I call a "theme" print. The person will try to find *exactly* the same colors that are in the print. If the print contains red, green, and blue, the person will buy only fabric that contains the exact color of red, green, or blue as in the multi-color print. This is very limiting. The results can also be very disappointing.

Someone who selects colors to exactly match a specific print usually wonders why the finished project looks dull. The colors looked so great in the multi-color fabric or wallpaper. Why does something seem lacking when those exact colors are then matched and used in a quilt? This chapter shows why this happens and how to avoid it. You'll learn how to create three types of palettes to coordinate with a theme print, each of which will result in a different look for your quilt. You can use these methods whether you are coordinating your project with an element in a room, such as upholstery or wallpaper, or whether you are actually using a theme print fabric in your quilt.

ILLUSTRATION 54 : *Notice the fine dark or black line in these multi-color fabrics.*

The Deep Dark—Easy to Miss

One reason a color scheme may seem lacking could be that not *all* of the colors in your theme print were selected! Take a look at each of the multi-colored large prints in illustration 54. In every case there is a fine very dark or black line outlining many of the colors.

When matching color prints such as these, it's easy to miss the black line. We tend not to see it because it is a thin outline and our eye does not perceive it as a color. Yet that line is as important to the overall look of the fabric as the tiny touch of deep dark is to your palette.

Illustration 55 shows renderings of two fabrics— what they look like with the dark line and what happens when that line is eliminated. Without the dark line they become dull and lose the depth that makes them complete. We don't realize when matching col-ors to a print that the dark line is what makes a particu-lar fabric look good, and the absence of the line makes the fabric look dull. That dark line will be discussed again later, but for now realize that the absence of that same type of dark in our quilts will make *them* look dull.

Theme Print Fabric as Guide, Not "God"

There is another reason something may seem lack-ing when colors are exactly matched to a theme print. The problem is that colors in shades darker and lighter, brighter and duller than the theme print are missing, and these would give so much more richness to the color scheme than having only exact matches. Select-ing colors from a multi-colored large print, a border

ILLUSTRATION 55 : *See what happens to these fabrics when the dark line is eliminated.*

print, wallpaper, or drapery fabric can be a great beginning for coordinating colors for a quilt. Working from a theme fabric can be a perfect guide for people who still feel unsure about color or who have a specific fabric or color scheme they would like to work around. If a particular print appeals to you and you like the colors, then you already know where to begin and can eliminate many of the fabrics in the shop. But that is just the point. It should only be a beginning. Don't use that fabric as "God" where no deviation can be made. Use it as a *guide*—find fabrics to match the main colors in the theme print, but then select whatever other colors are necessary to *shade* those fabrics together. The end result will be a much more interesting color scheme.

The Three Types of Coordinating Palettes

When creating a palette to go with a specific print design, there are three approaches you can take: You can match the print's colors exactly, you can use an expanded palette, or you can use a limited palette.

Look at the example of the paisley fabric shown in illustration 56. The fabric swatches of the palette beside it match exactly the colors in the print. While the colors look all right, the overall effect is not very exciting. The problem is that it lacks *shades* of any of the colors. There is a lavender, a blue, a green, and a peach, but only the taupe and the light brown belong to a similar color group. Furthermore, the black line out-

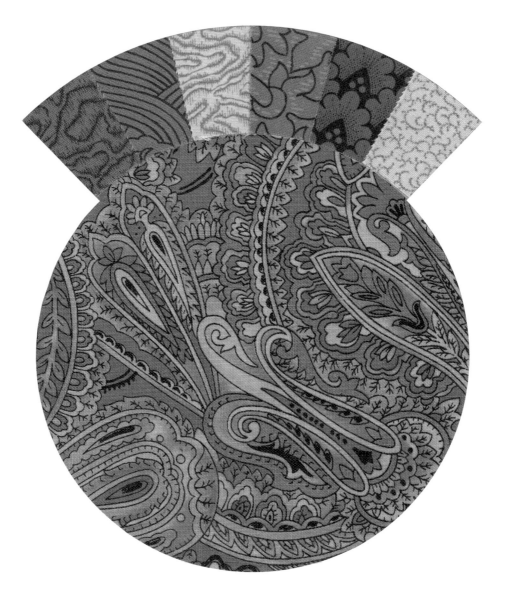

ILLUSTRATION 56: *Paisley print with exact match palette of colors.*

lining the colors was not perceived as a separate color and black has not been chosen.

Look now at illustration 57, where all of those colors shade together. The colors which have been added in order to blend from one color to the next add a dimension that changes a rather dull looking color scheme to one with much more vitality.

Therefore, my advice to anyone wishing to build a color scheme around a specific multi-color print is to exactly match all of the colors in the print, but don't stop there. Add whatever other colors are needed to

shade the original ones together, and the result will always be a beautiful combination of colors to use in a multi-color, multi-fabric quilt.

From the Expanded Palette to the Chosen Few

But as is the case with shaded palettes, that arrangement will most likely include between fifteen and

ILLUSTRATION 57 : *Paisley fabric with expanded palette of exact match colors shaded together.*

twenty-five colors. Many quilters will balk at this, as their preference might be to use no more than six to ten fabrics in a quilt. In this case, you would need to create a limited palette. Just as you saw how to pare down a palette in chapter 4, there is a step-by-step process by which you can create a smaller more limited palette designed around a specific print. Steps 1 and 2 will sound familiar; step 3 may surprise you, but it is the secret to creating a successful limited palette.

• STEP 1 • *Match the Colors*
The first step is to match all of the exact colors in the print, in effect creating the first palette described.

• STEP 2 • *Shade the Colors*
Second, create an expanded palette by shading the exact match colors together as in illustration 57.

• STEP 3 • *Eliminate Exact Matches*
The next step for selecting fewer colors is to *eliminate all of the colors that exactly match the print* (the swatches shown in illustration 56). You have seen how much more exciting a color combination is when there are several *shades* of the colors. So why use an exact color again when it is already in the theme print? When using only a few colors, don't restrict yourself by only matching the colors in the multi-colored print. This is too limiting. Take *advantage* of the print by letting *its* colors stand alone and have the other colors be *different* from those—a little brighter, duller, bolder, softer, and so on. Since so few colors will be used, this gives the opportunity of a more colorful quilt—the more variety the better. Illustration 58 shows the beginning of this process, with the exact match colors eliminated. Compare this illustration with the previous one. Has the

ILLUSTRATION 58 : *The exact match fabrics have been eliminated from the palette.*

impact of the colors been diminished at all? The impact is the *same* because all of the colors are still there! The eliminated ones still appear in the theme print.

• STEP 4 • *Work with Various Combinations*

Once the colors that exactly match the print have been eliminated, work with combinations of the remaining colors until you are happy with the result. Make sure you keep a deep dark and an accent. There are no specific "right" or "wrong" combinations. So much depends on which colors get emphasized and how dark or light you want the palette. The textural differences of the various fabrics may also play a role in your ultimate fabric choices. Illustrations 59A and 59B show two possible combinations. Both examples have shades of each of the original colors. But interestingly, the colors in the original shaded palette (illustration 57) that were the link or transition (fuchsia and pink) shading the lavender to the peach are what make the combinations work. Those pink tones are the only colors not in the original print. Illustration 59A contains the rose pink and 59B contains the

ILLUSTRATION 59A: *Two limited palettes coordinating with the paisley print.*
The transition color rose pink has been eliminated in the bottom palette.

ILLUSTRATION 59B : *Two limited palettes coordinating with the paisley print. The transition color fuchsia has been eliminated in the bottom palette.*

ILLUSTRATION 60: *Jungle print fabric with exact match colors.*

fuchsia. Without one of those transition colors both of the combinations become duller. In each of the illustrations the transition is included in the swatches on the top and eliminated in the ones on the bottom. Put your hand alternately over the swatches on the bottom and the top and see the difference with and without the transition.

The multi-colored jungle print fabric in illustrations 60 and 61 is a much darker and brighter one than that used in the preceding illustrations, but the same theory works. The swatches in the first illustration exactly match the colors in the print (illustration 60). When you look at those swatches with the print, even though the colors in the fabric are quite bright, the exact color match swatches appear a little dull. The main problem is a lack of accent (a brighter version of the general color range). Jay Romano chose this particular print for her quilt *Jungle Stars* (illustration 62). To create her expanded palette (illustration 61), she chose the exact match colors shown earlier and shaded those colors together, working down into the light tones to get her background color. Notice how much brighter the accent needs to be than the tones in the fabric itself. But as mentioned in the first chapter, everything is relative to the colors being used.

ILLUSTRATION 61: *Expanded palette created by shading those colors together.*

ILLUSTRATION 62 : Jungle Stars *quilt, made by Jay Romano.*

ILLUSTRATION 63 : *Limited palette made from expanded palette in illustration 61.*

To select fewer colors to coordinate with a large print such as the jungle print, follow the same principles as for the smaller paisley shown earlier: Eliminate the colors that exactly match the multi-color fabric and select others from the larger palette. One possible limited palette for the jungle print is shown in illustration 63.

Quilts Made Using Theme Print Fabrics

You've seen how to create the three types of coordinating palettes. Let's follow two series of quilts from beginning to end to see how the finished results differ.

Midnight Star *Series*

Let's suppose you've decided to make a quilt from the design *Midnight Star* shown in illustration 64, and you want to coordinate it around the border (theme) print shown here.

Many people would look at the design and the finished quilt and say that it seems there is room for a maximum of six different fabrics. Since the impact of the colors in the border fabric looks good, it will seem safe to exactly match those colors for the quilt. Therefore they would choose green, pink, beige, and two shades of blue to go with the border print. The print with these exact match colors is shown in illustration 65. However, most peo-

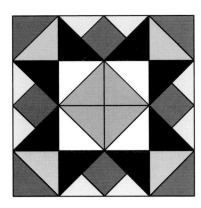

ILLUSTRATION 64 : Midnight Star *border print and block.*

ILLUSTRATION 65 : *Border print with exact match colors.*

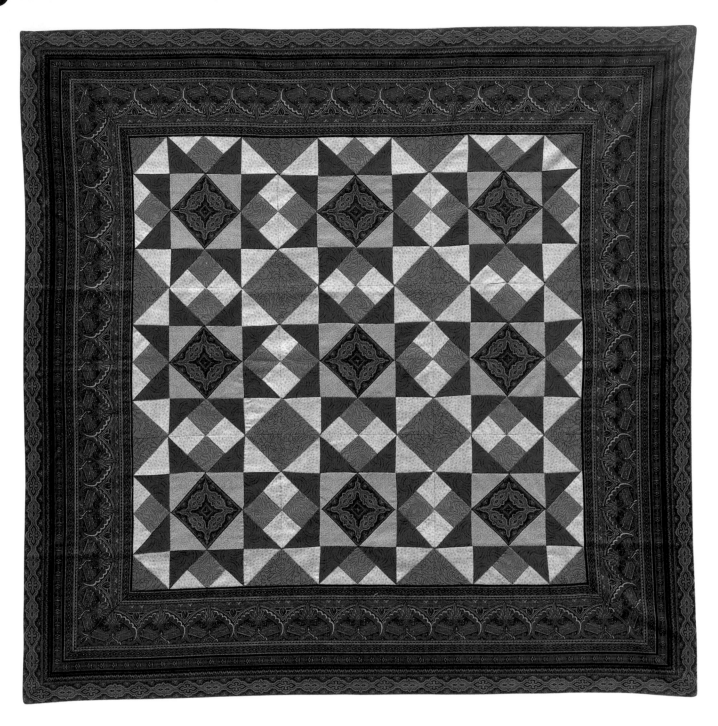

ILLUSTRATION 66 : Midnight Star *quilt using the blue and pink border print with exact match colors. All quilts in this series were designed by Jinny Beyer and made by Darlene Christopherson.*

ple would find the finished quilt (illustration 66) a little disappointing because it seems to lack some of the dimension that the fabric by itself had.

The reason is that once again the dark outline in the border print was not perceived as a color, which brings us back to the dark line that outlines many multi-color prints.

It is especially difficult for people to realize the importance of the dark line in a fabric such as this border print, because the black is simply not read as a color. The border print is the companion to the paisley print shown in illustration 67. Study the paisley, which is shown with and without the black line. If the black line were also removed from the border print it would appear as dull as the paisley fabric without the black line. Notice how the paisley fabric *without* the dark line more closely resembles the group of exact match fabrics chosen for the quilt.

ILLUSTRATION 67 : *Paisley fabric that is a companion to the blue border print. Notice how it becomes duller when the black line is eliminated.*

ILLUSTRATION 68 : *Palette created from shading the exact match colors together.*

Remember, exactly matching the colors in a favorite fabric is an excellent beginning, but don't stop there. The next step is to find a way to shade all of those colors together. Compare illustration 65 and illustration 68. You can see how much more exciting the colors become when the exact matched ones are shaded together.

Again, there are those who would say that the shaded colors look great, but the *Midnight Star* pattern can use a maximum of six different fabrics. Once more, this is a fallacy. As explained in chapter 4, many fabrics can be used effectively in a design such as this as long as some kind of continuity is maintained. For instance, you could plan for the points of the star to always be dark blue or dark teal and use many shades of dark blue and teal. The center square could always be made up of the border print, but it would be fun to work with as many variations of that border print as possible. The triangles outside the center square could always be green, but sometimes brighter green, sometimes duller. The squares between the points of the star could always be pink, but once again, several shades of pink from bright to dull. The background could always be light, but not always the same value of light. The corner triangles could always be a medium blue, but you could use several different shades and prints of medium blue.

Compare the quilt in illustration 69, where the expanded palette of all of the colors has been used, with the quilt in illustration 66 containing only the exact match colors.

ILLUSTRATION 69 : Midnight Star *quilt made from the expanded palette.*

ILLUSTRATION 70 : *Limited palette created from the
expanded palette.*

But what if you do not care for the "scrap look" created when so many fabrics are used and would still prefer to make a quilt where all blocks are of the same fabrics? How can this type of quilt be made with only a few fabrics, but still have more vitality? The process is similar to that described earlier in this chapter. Find the exact match of the colors in the theme print, shade all of those together, and finally start eliminating. Begin by eliminating all of the original matching fabrics. Then choose from the remaining swatches a light for a background, a favorite accent and the color you would most like to use for the deep dark. Continue working with the remaining swatches until you are satisfied with the balance of colors. Illustrations 70 and 71 show the six colors that were eventually chosen for the quilt and how they look made up into the same *Midnight Star* design.

Look at the three quilts in illustrations 66, 69, and 71 again. Which one do you like the best? Do not feel that it is "wrong" if you prefer the first quilt containing the exact matching colors. Some people like the orderliness that comes from having colors exactly match. People attracted to scrap quilts might like the second one with an expanded palette the best and yet others may prefer the third with the limited palette.

ILLUSTRATION 71: Midnight Star *quilt made from the limited palette.*

Rolling Star *Series*

Let's take a look at another example of quilts made using different types of palettes. The next three quilts based on this same concept use a different border print and *Rolling Star* as the block design. Fabrics that exactly match the border appear in illustration 72, and the resulting quilt made of these prints is shown in illustration 73.

Notice that the colors seem a little dull—there is no spark. That's because in attempting to exactly match the colors in the fabric, the black line was again not perceived as a separate color.

I was at the manufacturing plant when this particular fabric was being printed and asked if they could print a piece for me eliminating the last roller—the one containing the black line. When they brought me the piece of fabric I could not *believe* that it was the same

ILLUSTRATION 72 : *Border print with exact match colors.*

ILLUSTRATION 73 : Rolling Star *made from the exact match palette in illustration 72.*
All quilts in this series were designed by Jinny Beyer and made by Barb Celio.

design. The two versions of the fabric—with and without the black line—are shown in illustration 74. It will also be hard for *you* to believe that only the black line has been eliminated, but it's true! See how the quilt made from the exact match colors closely resembles the fabric swatch *without* the black line? This is what happens when the deep dark is lost.

A much more exciting palette can be created by shading those exact match colors together. There are many different ways that those particular colors could be shaded. I chose the one shown in illustration 75 with the olive greens, since it seemed less ordinary. The quilt using all the colors of that palette appears in illustration 76.

ILLUSTRATION 74 : *Border print used in* Rolling Star *quilts, printed with and without the black line.*

ILLUSTRATION 75 : *Palette created from exactly matching the colors in the border print and then shading them together.*

ILLUSTRATION 76 : Rolling Star *quilt made from the expanded palette shown in illustration 75.*

The third quilt (shown in illustration 78) also contains just a few colors, but those were chosen from the shaded palette, first by eliminating the exact match fabrics, and then by selecting others from those that remained. When creating the limited palette for this quilt (shown in illustration 77), care was taken to choose an accent (bright red), a deep dark (navy), and then other colors to give a balance. When you go through the process of creating a palette this way, you'll see how much easier it is to select colors from the palette than to look at a print and try to visualize what colors will go with it.

ILLUSTRATION 77 : *Limited palette using colors selected from illustration 75.*

ILLUSTRATION 78 : Rolling Star *quilt made from the limited palette shown in illustration 77.*

Hound's Tooth Square *Quilt*

In this last example, Judy Spahn wanted to use just a few fabrics in her quilt *Hound's Tooth Square*, shown in illustration 79, but she maximized the color impact by selecting some multi-color fabrics containing several of the colors she wanted to use. She began with the large bold jungle theme print and chose colors that exactly matched that print. Those colors are shown on the top portion of illustration 80.

Next she shaded the colors together; her expanded palette is shown in illustration 81.

ILLUSTRATION 79 : Hound's Tooth Square, *made by Judy Spahn.*

ILLUSTRATION 80: *Print around which Judy selected colors and fabrics for her quilt*
Hound's Tooth Square. *Colors that exactly match the print are on the top.*
The fabrics Judy selected for her quilt are on the bottom.

ILLUSTRATION 81: *Expanded palette, shaded from exact match colors.*

Judy did not want her quilt to contain as many fabrics as are represented in the expanded palette, but wanted as many of the *colors* as possible. She did not need any fabrics in colors that exactly matched her theme print since those colors were already so prominent. She was able to find two other multi-color prints that gave her several of the other colors—the brighter olive green, gold, purple tones, and so on. For the accent she chose the brighter coral and for the background the lavender and taupe.

Look at illustration 80. The fabrics at the bottom are the ones Judy selected for her quilt. Notice the rich quality that is achieved by the variety of textures in the prints. Then refer to the quilt and see how much impact those textures have on the entire design.

Put your hand over Judy's swatches and look at the exact match fabrics on the top and how they relate to the theme print. Now put your hand on the exact match swatches and look at the theme print with Judy's swatches at the bottom of the circle. Compare those with the expanded palette in illustration 81. The color impact in Judy's palette is still there because so many of the colors from the expanded palette have been picked up in the fabrics she selected.

EXERCISE 8

Coordinating Fabrics with Theme Prints

Now it's time to use these principles to practice on your own.

• STEP 1 • *Select a Print*

Select from your fabric collection a large-scale multi-color print. If you do not have any, choose wallpaper or drapery or upholstery fabric from somewhere in your house. Or, choose one of the six multi-color prints shown in illustration 54 of this chapter.

• STEP 2 • *Match the Colors*

Select the exact match colors from your loose paper or fabric swatches. While you may prefer this type of palette, for practice go on to step 3.

• STEP 3 • *Shade the Colors*

Next, make an expanded palette. Add whatever other swatches you need to shade those exact match colors together. Make sure the colors blend smoothly from one to the next.

• STEP 4 • *Pare Down the Colors*

You may prefer the expanded palette, but just for practice see what happens when you create a limited palette by paring it down to six or eight colors. Begin by eliminating the exact match colors; then work with the remaining swatches to find a balance of color. Make sure to include an accent and a deep dark.

• STEP 5 • *Find Fabrics for the Palette*

Look through your fabric collection and find fabrics to correspond to the swatches in your palette. Then work with them to find a balance in the textures of the prints as well as the color.

Repeat this exercise with at least four more large-scale multi-color prints.

Chapter **6** PALETTE PRACTICE WITH QUILTS

This chapter will provide you with some clear cut guidelines on how to use your palette in creating actual quilts. By now you should be feeling confident about your ability to coordinate colors, but it may still seem a little overwhelming to actually put those colors into a design in a meaningful manner. When beginning a new quilting project, I follow the steps outlined below. These guidelines will also help you begin your next quilt.

Designing and Making a Quilt

• STEP 1 • *Select a Quilt Pattern*

Often I will have a specific quilt pattern in mind that I would like to use. Other times I will design a new one or pore through books looking for ones that will inspire me. This chapter contains templates for several quilts and variations of those designs. I chose these quilt patterns because I felt they would give you some good palette practice. If you do not yet have a specific pattern of your own in mind, simply choose one of these patterns and jump right in!

• STEP 2 • *Find a Unit*

With *any* quilt design I look for a repeat unit that I can use for both designing and sewing. In a repeat block quilt such as the *Rolling Star* quilts shown in illustrations 73, 76, and 78 the unit would be a single block. In a quilt with an all-over pattern such as the

Tumbling Blocks (see illustration 88), a unit can be created by putting several diamonds together to form a larger diamond, or a hexagon (see illustration 86).

When making a quilt some people plan in advance by working with colored pencils, or they actually put pieces of fabric on a wall and have everything completely decided before beginning to sew. These techniques don't work for me because it's hard for me to visualize in advance the exact proportion of certain colors that I want to use and their exact placement in the quilt.

Instead, when a few of the individual units in the quilt are completed, I place them on a floor or wall and study them. Sometimes I will look at them and realize that when the units are placed side by side the overall effect may be too dark, too bright, or not bright enough. Maybe the prints all appear too similar or perhaps I wanted a blue and green quilt, with more emphasis on the blue, but now there appears to be more green.

If you work in units, with each unit remaining separate until they are all complete, you can make adjustments in the remaining units as the quilt progresses. If the first ones seem too dark, you do not have to take them apart or discard them—simply make the next units minus the really dark colors. The next time the units are laid out you can intersperse the darker ones with the lighter ones, and the darkness becomes diffused. If the first few units appear dull, make some of the next ones with brighter accents. If the prints all appear too solid, make new units concentrating more on a variety of textures. As you work with the units you will begin to get a feel for how to balance the various elements discussed in this book and how to use your palette of colors. If you practice incorporating the principles of shading all of your colors, then the deep dark, and the accent will become almost second nature.

• STEP 3 • *Design in Black and White*

All of my quilt designing is first done in black and white, and I recommend that you work this way too. Once you have selected a design and found a workable "unit," make several line drawings of that unit (or make one drawing and photocopy it several times). Using a graphite pencil or a black marker, shade different portions of the design in as many variations as possible. Concentrate on dark, medium, and light placement. The *Rolling Star* block is shown in illustration 82 with three variations in shading.

Once the units have been shaded in many different ways, photocopy the page several times, cut out the units, and paste them together with all of the same units side by side. You'll be amazed to see how different the designs can look, just by changing the dark, medium, and light placement. The *Rolling Star* blocks from illustration 82 have been copied and the like units put together in illustration 83.

Creating a black and white illustration of the design in this manner gives you the opportunity to determine where the dark, medium, and light colored fabrics will go in the quilt. You can later sort your fabrics into dark, medium, and light colored piles. Please note, however, that dark, medium, and light are relative to the other fabrics being used. In the *Tumbling Blocks* quilt shown in illustration 88 the light fabric on the tops of the blocks only has to be lighter than the dark and medium diamonds around it in order for your eye to still perceive it as light.

ILLUSTRATION 82 : Rolling Star *shaded in three different ways.*

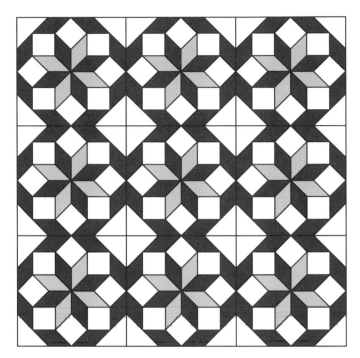

ILLUSTRATION 83 : Rolling Star *blocks that have been shaded different ways, photocopied, and placed side by side.*

• S T E P 4 • *Plan the Size of the Quilt*

You should have a fairly good idea about how large you want your quilt to be and whether or not there will be a border. On a full-size quilt, plan approximately 10″ to 12″ (25.4cm to 30.5cm) per side for the width of a border. I never know exactly how wide the border will be until I get to that point, because I find it impossible to plan a border until the rest of the quilt is finished. But you can more or less guess that a border will take up 20″ to 25″ (50.8cm to 63.5cm) of the total width and length of the quilt.

Next, decide how many units will fill up the rest of the space. In block style quilts, I usually like to have an odd number of blocks. That way one block can be centered in the middle of the bed, which seems visually more pleasing. If you are working with a ready made pattern, you will be limited as to the size of the quilt, since you can only increase or decrease the quilt dimensions by the size of the unit or block. As an alternative, you may choose to draft your own pattern in the size that will give you the number of units you prefer for the size of the quilt.

• S T E P 5 • *(Optional) Draft the Pattern and Make the Templates*

The next step is to draft your pattern in the size you want your block or unit to be and then make the templates. If you are using one of the patterns in this book, you will not need to draft the pattern unless you want it to be a different size than the ones given here. The patterns in this chapter are given *without* seam allowance. Therefore if you use one of them you *must* remember to *add 1/4″ (6 mm) seam allowance around all sides of all pieces.*

Once the black and white units have been put together, I often decide it makes sense to alter the pattern. For example in the *Rolling Star* illustrations, when the blocks are joined, the triangles in the corner of the blocks form a square. Sometimes I may leave them as triangles and experiment with different fabrics in those corners. But other times, particularly if the same fabric will be used in all corners, I may simplify the pattern and eliminate the triangles and make one large square for the corners. This would affect the pattern and the templates would have to be altered accordingly.

• S T E P 6 • *Create a Palette of Colors*

It is usually at this stage in the process of a quilt design that I create a palette of colors for a quilt. I may already have had specific colors in mind, or a particular fabric that I wanted to work with, but now is the time to get those ideas consolidated. Prior to developing my color system, I never created a palette before beginning a quilt. After starting the quilt, I found myself constantly making changes in what had already been sewn because the colors did not seem just right. Since working with this system and designing the palette in advance, I find that I no longer am dissatisfied with the colors and can proceed with confidence in the making of the quilt.

I create an individual palette for each quilt and mount it on a piece of cardboard, which will then be a handy reference as I select fabrics and work on the quilt.

• S T E P 7 • *Gather the Fabrics*

By now you are well aware of the fact that I like to incorporate many fabrics in my quilts, preferring the look that is created by using many different prints and many shades of the colors in the selected color scheme. Therefore you can probably guess my philosophy about providing fabric charts for the quilt patterns given in this book. How can I tell you how much fabric to purchase for a particular quilt when I don't know how much I would use myself? Even if I decide to always make the points of a particular star blue, I would not use the same blue fabric throughout, but would probably incorporate several different blues— some with different textures, others a little darker or lighter or brighter.

Once you have created the basic palette for the quilt, find fabrics from your own collection that will work into that color scheme. If you have been trying to gather a selection of fabrics that covers the color spectrum, chances are that you will already have on hand a large proportion of the colors needed for your quilt. In many cases, you will need to take the palette to the fabric shop and look for additional ones that will coordinate. If you plan to use many different fabrics, it is not necessary to purchase a lot of any particular print. One-fourth to one-half yard (or meter) should be sufficient. For continuity you might plan to select one fabric that will be used in the same place throughout the quilt. If this is the case, make a template, see how many of those will fit onto a quarter yard (or meter) of fabric and then multiply it by the number of pieces you will need to find the amount of fabric to purchase.

One of the nice things about using many different fabrics in a quilt is that if you run out of one fabric, all you need to do is to find another one in a similar color and use that one in its place.

If many different fabrics are incorporated into a quilt, the only fabric you have to be sure to have enough of is that used for long border pieces. That is not usually a problem for me either since I never plan a border until the main body of the quilt is finished. I never know what border will look the best until all of the blocks are put together. So, I often purchase some of the fabrics I use in the borders at a later time.

• STEP 8 • *Place the Colors Within the Quilt*
Once the fabric has been gathered for a project, you

are ready to begin. The next decision is how you want to "color" the quilt. Basically you will either *shade* the colors and fabrics, creating units by color or gradation, or you may choose to *scatter* the colors of your palette throughout the quilt. The quilts shown throughout this book use both methods. For instance *Borealis* on page 67, and *Vasarely II, Autumn Pond, Building Blocks,* and *Rolling Star* (illustrations in this chapter) are all done with each unit shaded from dark to light in one direction or the other. The *Rolling Star, Midnight Star, Mariner's Compass,* and *Tumbling Blocks* (illustrations 76, 69, 49, 88) have the colors on the palette placed more randomly throughout the quilt. The patterns given in this chapter have been developed to provide you with opportunities to use both of these approaches.

The Quilt Patterns and their Variations

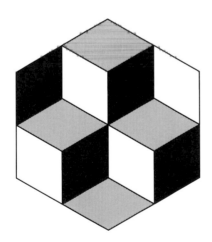

60° Diamond *Pattern*

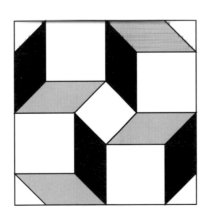

Building Blocks *Pattern*

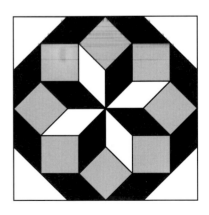

Rolling Star *Pattern*

On the following pages I provide you with three basic quilt patterns (shown above) and their variations: a total of 11 designs in all. The first, based on the 60° diamond, includes four variations—two of which were designed and made by first-time quilters! The second pattern, Building Blocks, is based on a square block that you can repeat to form a quilt, or "fragment" for a completely different look. Four variations of this pattern are shown. Finally, the Rolling Star pattern has three variations, including one created by "fragmenting" the basic unit.

PATTERNS BASED ON THE 60° DIAMOND
Four Variations

Without a doubt the 60° diamond is my favorite shape to work with in patchwork, and it is one of the least intimidating patterns for a beginning quiltmaker. When people indicate to me an interest in quilting, and don't quite know where to begin, I always urge them to begin with a quilt (why waste time on a series of small projects, when a quilt is the end goal?). Next I bring out a picture of a *Tumbling Blocks* quilt and ask how they feel about starting with that pattern. They usually like it and so we get started right away. I choose this design because it is not necessary to make all of the decisions at once, it is easy to piece, requires basically one single template, and you can work in units, getting a feel for the colors, textures, and contrasts as you work.

Variation I: Tumbling Blocks

Robin Morrison has been a longtime friend, watching me quilt from afar. One day, she indicated to me that she would like to try making a quilt, but didn't know how to begin. I suggested that she begin by choosing a design and showed her the *Tumbling Blocks* (illustration 84A). She liked it, so we drafted the pattern first making a hexagon and then breaking that into three identical diamonds (illustration 84B). We then used the diamonds as a basis for creating the templates (illustration 85). I explained that the diamond is the piece used for the basic pattern (piece A) and that she would need to use different templates around the edges of the quilt—the diamond cut in half *lengthwise* (piece B) is used along the top and bottom edges; the diamond cut in half *sideways* (piece C) is used on the other two edges; and then piece C is divided in half again for the corners (piece D).

I next showed Robin how to put the diamonds together to form a unit and how, within that unit, she needed to decide upon the placement of darks, mediums, and lights. I explained that once the units were pieced, they would all have to be oriented in the same direction when they were put together so that the dark, medium, and light placement would remain constant throughout. Once those units are put to-

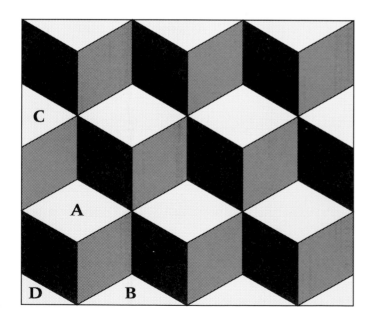

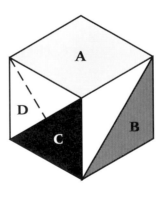

ILLUSTRATION 84A and B: *Diagram of* Tumbling Blocks *design, and the hexagon used to draft the templates.*

gether, the unit appears to vanish completely and just the tumbling blocks are visible. The completed unit is shown in illustration 86. The templates given here will produce a unit with a finished size of 8″ (20.3cm) from straight side to side and 9″ (22.9cm) from point to point.

Robin told me that she liked red, blue, and purple and would like to use those colors in her quilt. I explained a little about my color system to her, especially the importance of shading and gave her one of my Portable Palettes® (see Resource section) to look through. She found specific red, blue, and purple swatches that she particularly liked. Then I sent her home with the Portable Palette® and told her to come back when she had all of those colors shaded together in a smooth-flowing palette with no jumps between dark and light, or from one color to the next. Her beginning colors and shaded palette, along with her very first quilt are shown in illustrations 87 and 88.

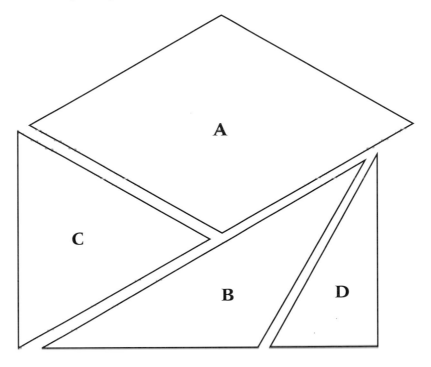

ILLUSTRATION 85 : *60° diamond templates.*
Note: Add 1/4″ (6mm) seam allowance around all sides of all templates.

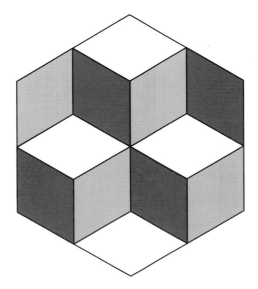

ILLUSTRATION 86 : *Unit to use for piecing the* Tumbling Blocks *design.*

ILLUSTRATION 87 : *Palette shading red, blue, and purple, which Robin Morrison used in her* Tumbling Blocks *quilt.*

ILLUSTRATION 88: Tumbling Blocks, *made by*
Robin Morrison.

ILLUSTRATION 89 : Vasarely II, *made by Jinny Beyer and quilted by Toni Smith.*

Variation II: Vasarely II and Autumn Pond

Another friend, Jeff Bartee, was visiting me and indicated an interest in beginning a quilt. He told me he liked quilts with depth and optical illusion qualities. I once again went to the 60° diamond, but I showed him how I put the diamond in a different type of unit, in the small quilt *Vasarely II,* shown in illustration 89.

In this quilt nine diamonds were put together to form a larger diamond, with the units shaded dark to light lengthwise or sideways. The units themselves were then stacked like *Tumbling Blocks,* except sometimes two blocks were placed on top of each other before a top was added. See illustration 90, which shows the shaded units, and illustration 91, which shows the overall placement of units. Notice also how half units are used to fill in and square off the edges.

I felt that this was a good project for a beginner because the initial task is just to sew individual units to the maker's satisfaction, shading colors within the units according to the original shading diagram.

Jeff said he liked really bold colors and would like to make a wall-hanging for his home. He had decorated a room with a fabric that included red, yellow, orange, blue, khaki, and gold, and wanted to use these colors. He expressed concern that it might not be possible to use all of those colors together in a quilt. I told him that anything was possible as long as the colors were shaded together. Through shading, he would be forced to add colors he might not have thought of, yet were important to the completion of the color scheme. It was the addition of the purples and browns that tied all the colors together. His completed quilt and palette of colors are shown in illustrations 92 and 93. Notice how Jeff varied the placement of the units in his quilt, *Autumn Pond,* and created a larger hexagon instead of a rectangle as in *Vasarely II.* The fabric around which he developed his color scheme has been used for the border of the quilt.

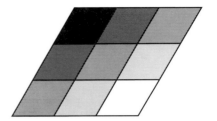

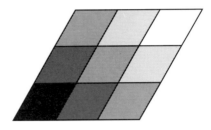

ILLUSTRATION 90: *How the units were shaded for* Vasarely II.

ILLUSTRATION 91: *How the units were placed in the design for* Vasarely II.

ILLUSTRATION 92 : *Palette used for making* Autumn Pond.

ILLUSTRATION 93 : Autumn Pond, *made by Jeff Bartee.*

Variation III: Bound to Be Charming

Jennifer Heffernan used the same basic unit as was used in the previous two quilts —nine diamonds forming a larger diamond—but she *shaded* the diamonds differently for her charm quilt, shown in illustration 94. A charm quilt is one in which each piece is cut from a different fabric. All in all Jennifer has 930 different pieces in her quilt, including the binding—thus its name *Bound to Be Charming*. Nevertheless with all of the fabrics pieced into the quilt Jennifer has still maintained her palette of colors, which is shown in illustration 95.

In variation II there are subtle differences between the diamonds as they are gradually shaded, but in Jennifer's version the design comes from a strong light/dark contrast. The shaded unit, along with the way those units were placed together are shown in illustration 96.

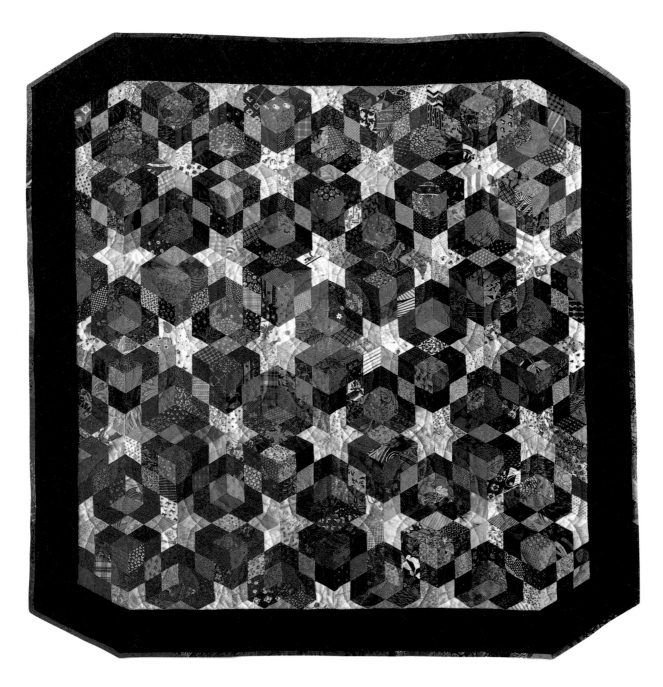

ILLUSTRATION 94 : Bound to Be Charming, *made by Jennifer Heffernan.*

ILLUSTRATION 95 : *Palette of colors used for*
Bound to Be Charming.

ILLUSTRATION 96 : *Shaded unit (right) and unit placement (left) for*
Bound to Be Charming, *the quilt in illustration 94.*

Variation IV: Jungle Stars

Jay Romano used the 60° diamond along with the half diamond (pattern pieces A and C from illustration 85), and the hexagon (E) and larger triangle (F and G) templates shown in illustration 98, to create her quilt, *Jungle Stars*, which is shown in illustration 62. Using the palette she made working with the jungle print, she pieced a variety of six-pointed stars. Some of the stars were made up only of diamonds, others had a hexagon in the center with points out of the triangles (half diamonds, piece C), and still others had stars pieced of all triangles (see illustration 97). In all cases, diamonds (piece A) were sewn between the points of the stars to create a larger hexagon unit. This unit is the same size, 8″ by 9″ (20.3cm by 22.9cm), as the hexagon unit in the *Tumbling Blocks* variation shown in illustration 86. The star units were then set with the large triangle (F) in between them (illustration 97), which gives an interesting illusion of small stars within larger stars.

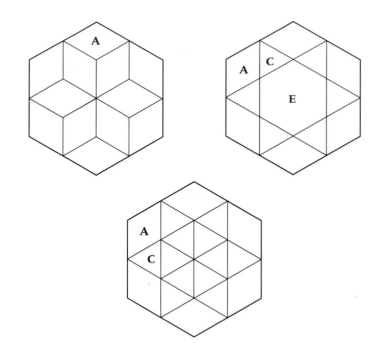

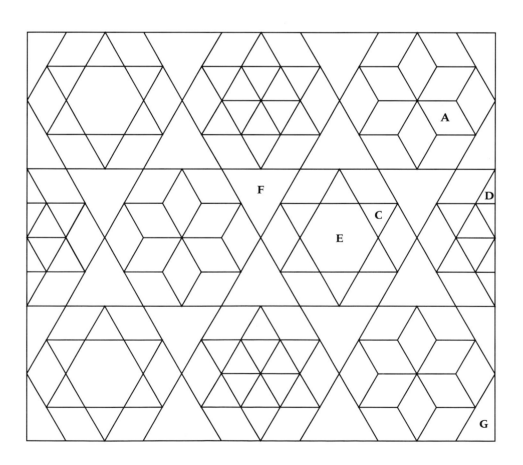

ILLUSTRATION 97 : *Star variations made from 60° diamonds used in* Jungle Stars *quilt and overall layout of design.*

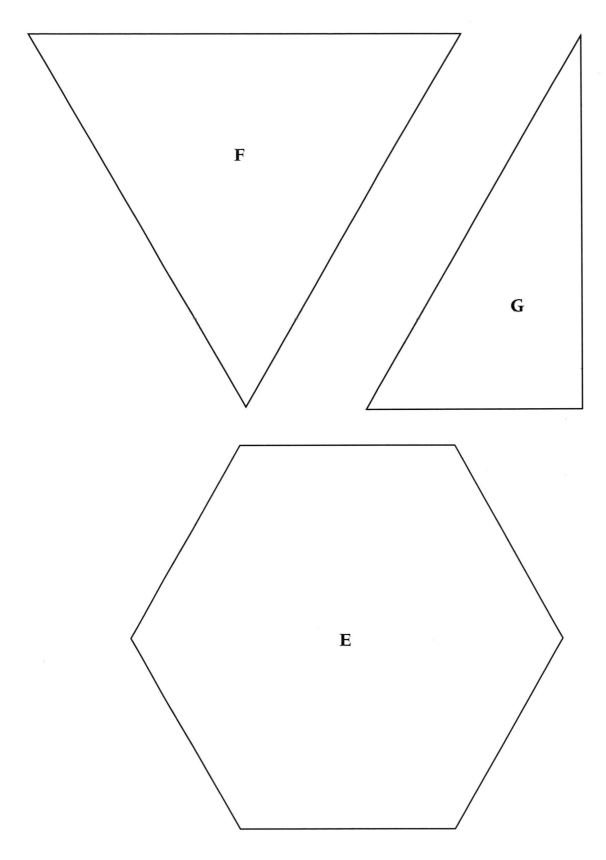

ILLUSTRATION 98: *Additional templates needed for*
Jungle Stars *quilt. Note: Add 1/4" (6mm) seam allowance to all*
sides of each template.

BUILDING BLOCKS

Four Variations

Building Blocks is another design that offers a variety of possibilities both for design and color manipulation.

Variation I: Building Blocks

The templates given in illustration 99 for the basic block are for an 8″ (20.3cm) square. Note: When cutting fabric pieces from template no. 2, the parallelogram, cut four pieces one way and the other four with the template reversed.

Copy the line drawing of the block design and shade it in as many ways as you can think of. Then make multiple photocopies of each, put them together and see which shaded version you prefer. One version is shown in illustration 100 with nine blocks put together. Notice that where the corners join, a square is formed of the small triangles. I would probably piece that as a single square (pattern piece 3), rather than four triangles.

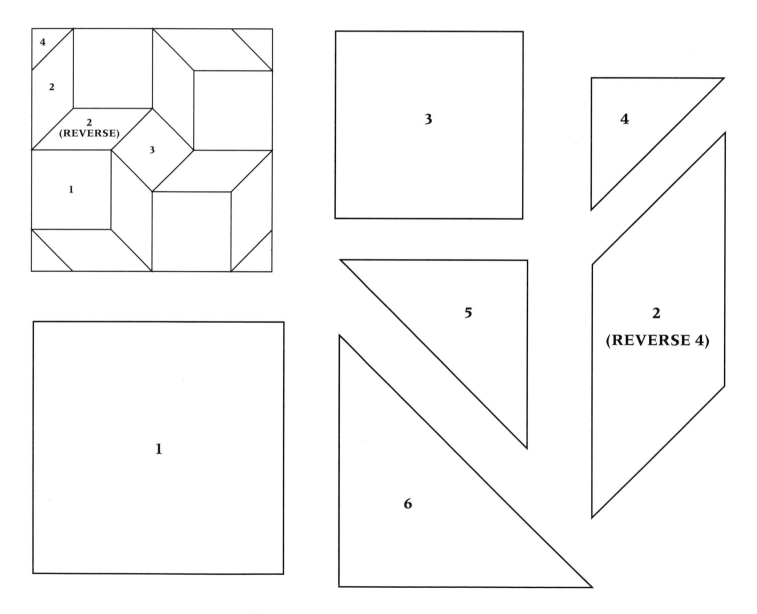

ILLUSTRATION 99 : *Diagram of* Building Blocks *and templates.*
Note: Add 1/4″ (6mm) seam allowance to all sides of all templates.

ILLUSTRATION 100 : *One possible shaded variation of* Building Blocks.

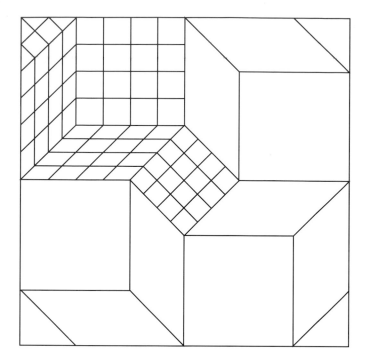

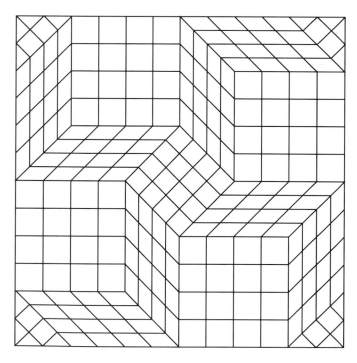

ILLUSTRATION 101: *Line drawing of partially fragmented block and fully fragmented block. This version divides each unit four times, breaking them down into 16 pieces each.*

Variation II: A Single Fragmented Block

Another interesting variation of the *Building Blocks* pattern is to create a single block, make it very large and then "fragment" the pieces by breaking the square into smaller squares, the parallelogram into smaller parallelograms, and so on as shown in illustration 101.

In order to fragment a design you do not need to draft a *larger* size of the design and break it down. Rather, you draft a *workable* size of the basic design, and *build it up* to the size you want, in effect, creating "divisions" in the process. After you draft the basic design, you use those same templates for the fragmented version as well. In fact, the same templates for variation I were used for variation II.

To begin, decide how large you want the quilt to be; that will determine how many divisions you will break each unit into, and therefore how many of each parallelogram, square, and triangle pieces will go into each unit. For example, if you are going to use the 8" square (20.3cm) pattern for *Building Blocks* given in illustration 99, three divisions of each side of a fragmented unit would use each template nine times, and give a finished block 24" (81cm) square. Four divisions would use each template sixteen times per unit and would produce a finished 32" (81.3cm) square. Five divisions will make a 40" (101.6cm) square and six divisions will make a 48" (121.9cm) square. When this design was fragmented, I felt that the corner triangles were too small, so I made a square and triangles in the corners instead (pattern pieces no. 3 and 5), giving the illusion of another square beginning to emerge. The fragmented version of this design is shown in a line drawing in illustration 101. Two quilts made in different color combinations of this variation appear in illustrations 102 and 103.

If you would like to make this variation, the first step is to copy the line drawing in illustration 101 and shade each unit in as many different ways as you can. In this case the units are large fragmented parallelograms, triangles, and squares. Notice how the units were shaded in the quilts in illustrations 102 and 103. Use these quilts as a guide as you experiment with shading dark to light from point to point, sideways, and so on. Once you have shaded the units, photocopy and cut them apart and remake the design until you find a shaded version you prefer. Then, working with your palette begin piecing the units, shading light to dark according to your diagram.

ILLUSTRATION 102 : Building Blocks Variation, *a fragmented design using three divisions, made by Jinny Beyer, and quilted by Toni Smith.*

ILLUSTRATION 103 : Building Blocks Variation, *using three divisions, made by Jinny Beyer and quilted by Toni Smith.*

Variation III: Four Fragmented Blocks

Another possibility is to put two or more fragmented blocks together. The drawing in illustration 104 shows four fragmented blocks, each consisting of four divisions. This would produce a finished piece without borders of 64 inches (162.6cm) square.

ILLUSTRATION 104 : *Four fragmented blocks of* Building Blocks *put together.*

Variation IV: Boxes and Stars

Look again at the two blue quilts, *Boxes and Stars*, shown in illustrations 27 and 29. The same templates for *Building Blocks* (page 118) can be used for this variation. The line drawing in illustration 105 indicates which templates to use for this design.

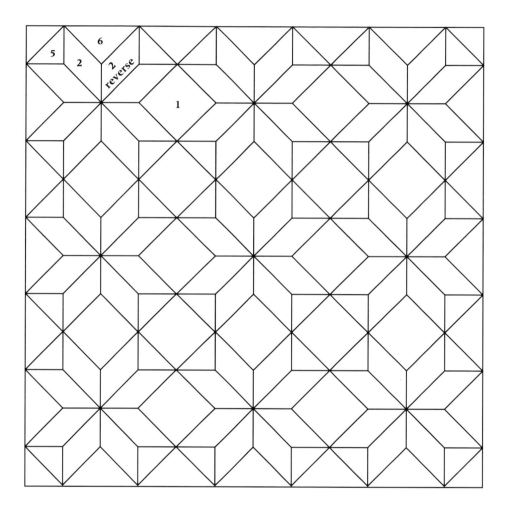

ILLUSTRATION 105 : *Line drawing of* Boxes and Stars *variation showing which templates to use and how the units fit together.*

ROLLING STAR

Three Variations

The *Rolling Star* pattern also offers many possibilities for working with color and design. Only three templates, a diamond (a), square (b), and triangle (c) are needed for the basic block (see illustration 106). The template patterns given here will produce a 9 1/2" (24.1cm) block.

Variation I: Rolling Star

Look again at the three *Rolling Star* quilts shown in illustrations 73, 76 and 78. You may want to execute this design using either an expanded palette and "scattering" the colors, or using a limited palette with each color used consistently as explained in previous chapters. (Also look again at pages 102 and 103 to see how different this design looks, depending on how it is shaded.) Using the multiple photocopy technique, experiment with shading the line drawing to find the variation you prefer.

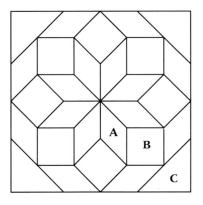

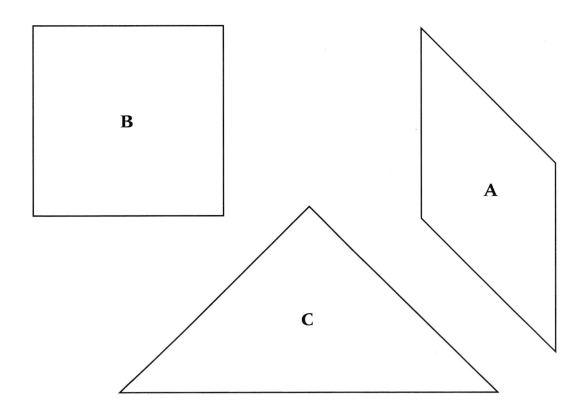

ILLUSTRATION 106: Rolling Star *block and templates.*
Note: Add 1/4" (6mm) seam allowance to all sides of all templates.

Variation II: A Single Fragmented Block

Another possibility for this design is to fragment it as was done in the *Building Blocks* variation II. A line drawing appears in illustration 107 for you to copy and shade. Once again, think of as many different ways as possible to shade the various units, then photocopy and rebuild the design. The quilt made by Kathy Light Smith shown in illustration 108 shows just one possibility for shading and making a fragmented *Rolling Star* quilt.

The same templates given for the basic *Rolling Star* block (illustration 106) can be used for this variation. Since the original design is 9 1/2" (24.1cm), if you fragment each shape three times, the finished block will be 28 1/2" (72.4cm); four times will be 38" (96.5cm) square; five times produces a 47 1/2" (120.7cm) square; and six times will give a 57" (144.8cm) quilt.

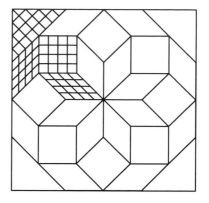

ILLUSTRATION 107: *Partially and fully fragmented blocks of* Rolling Star.

ILLUSTRATION 108 : *Fragmented* Rolling Star *quilt, made by
Kathy Light Smith.*

Variation III: Four Fragmented Blocks

Here again you may want to put four fragmented blocks together for a large quilt as in illustra-tion 109. This variation uses four divisions of each unit and would produce a finished size of 57" (144.8cm) square.

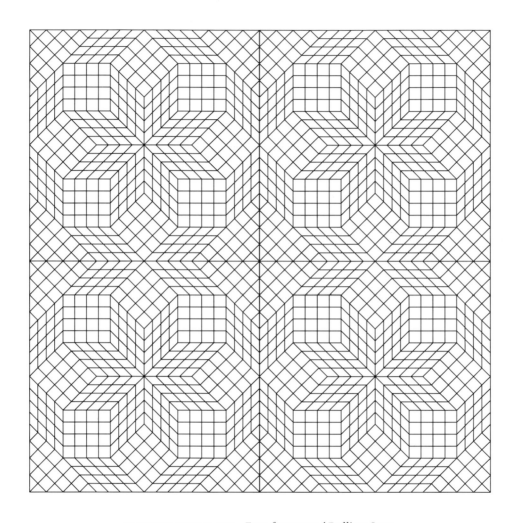

ILLUSTRATION 109 : *Four fragmented* Rolling Star
blocks joined together.

Enjoy Your New Color Confidence

Whichever pattern you choose to begin your first palette project, it is my hope that the information presented in this book has helped you to feel much more confident about working with color in not only your quilts, but also in other areas where you make decisions on color. Remember that it is not the colors initially chosen for a project, but what is *added* to those colors that makes all the difference. Select colors that *you* like and want to work with, not ones you think others would approve of. A quilt is an individual expression of yourself and I hope this book has helped you gain the confidence to be true to yourself and to express what you feel and believe.

SUGGESTIONS FOR TEACHERS

This book can be used as a textbook, with students following the exercises under your guidance. Students can work with the paper swatches in the book, you can prepare fabric swatches for them to work with, or you can order sets of fabric swatches for them to use (see Resources). Some possible ways to organize classes—depending on how many hours or days you want the class to be—are given here. Each exercise detailed in the various chapters has been listed below along with the average time it takes students in my classes to complete the exercise. I have also given some examples or ways in which I work with these various exercises.

Sample items that would be helpful for you to bring to class include:

• **MASTER PALETTE** • One you have made that is large enough to display is best, but you could refer students to the two sample palettes in the book.

• **A PORTABLE PALETTE®** • A helpful ready-made tool for showing shading, holding up swatches, and so forth (See Resources).

• **SAMPLE QUILTS** • It would be useful to have at least one quilt sample to show, as well as the color palette that was used to make it.

• **THEME PRINT FABRICS** • These are needed in case students forget to bring one and you want to demonstrate how to coordinate colors with a print.

Teaching the Exercises

EXERCISE 1

Creating Your Master Palette

Approximate time for exercise—1 hour and 45 minutes.

I begin all of my color classes with this exercise. I start by briefly holding up one of my master palettes to show how the shading should flow. (Don't leave this on display, or some people will think that is the way it *should* be and will try to copy it.) I give the basic instructions concerning sorting by color and gray tones, and the fact that they can shade the swatches into a circle or leave two ends open and that they can leave up to two swatches out.

When they have finished the shading they tape or glue one side of the swatches to their posterboard and cut off one-third of each to use for other exercises.

Then I spend about 20 minutes explaining my color system and the importance of shading, the deep dark, and the accent. I show some quilts I have made along with the palettes they were made from; you could have them turn to the quilts and the related palettes in this book.

EXERCISE 2

Consider the Possibilities

Approximate time for exercise—15 minutes.

You can have students do this exercise using my Portable Palette®, the sample master palettes in this book, the master palettes they have made, or with all three types of palettes. This exercise allows students to see how many beautiful color combinations there are.

EXERCISE 3

Shading Two Colors Together

Approximate time for teacher explanation and demonstration—10 minutes.
Approximate time for student work—10 minutes per set of colors.

I begin this exercise by showing a master palette and asking students to select two colors from the palette that they think would look terrible together. I pull both of those colors out of my Portable Palette® hold them up and then proceed to shade them together in front of the class. The class is always amazed at how good the colors look when they are shaded together.

Next, they can use Portable Palettes® or loose swatches to shade two colors; I usually have them work in two or three person groups. Once the groups have completed the exercise, then have everyone in the class see the results of each group. The students will immediately see how many *different* ways two colors can be shaded together.

After they shade one set of colors together as a group, have them do sets on their own.

EXERCISE 4

Shading Three Colors Together

Approximate time for exercise—10 to 15 minutes per set of colors.

Proceed as for exercise 3.

EXERCISE 5

Working with a Monochromatic Color Scheme

Approximate time for exercise—10 minutes.

Follow as explained in book.

EXERCISE 6

How Much Variety in Your Prints?

Approximate time for exercise—20 minutes.

I use this exercise in classes where students have brought many of their fabrics to class. After explaining about the different types of textures in prints, I give them several pages of swatches of fabrics that have been photocopied and ask them to find and cut out twelve completely different textures from the handout sheets. I have made certain to have a wide variety of textures but also include many fabrics of similar textures.

After they find twelve different textures in the handouts, I have them turn to their own fabrics and find 12 different textures in those (they are not to worry about color, only the print). This is a valuable exercise as many people now discover that they have been purchasing similar types of prints.

EXERCISE 7

Selecting Fewer Colors from a Larger Palette

Approximate time for exercise—15 minutes.

I often teach this exercise directly after exercises 3 or 4. Follow as explained in Chapter 4.

EXERCISE 8

Coordinating Fabrics with Theme Prints

Approximate total time for exercise—45 minutes
  Teacher time—15 minutes
  Group exercise—15 minutes
  Individual exercise—15 minutes

If this exercise is going to be a part of the color class (it is in every color class I teach) I work with sets of quilts similar to the *Midnight Star* and *Rolling Star* quilt sets shown on pages 84 through 90. Before class I put these on a wall and number each set. As students arrive I ask them to take a piece of paper and vote for the quilt in each set that they like the best. Then as they make their master palette, I tally the votes and later, as I explain my color system and begin to talk about the "matching syndrome" I use those quilts as examples.

It would be helpful for you to make a similar set of quilts working from your own theme print, or at least have the students turn to each set in this book and vote on them. I like for the students to vote before class begins because you find out their true reactions. Interestingly enough, the voting is almost always the same. In a class of twenty-five students, two or three will vote for the quilt that exactly matches the print, and the rest of the students will be evenly divided between the other two.

I recommend that students first do the exercise as a two or three person group. I bring to class 1/2 yard pieces of several different multi-color theme prints and give one to each group. Working with a Portable Palette® or one of the students' loose swatches they are to do the exercise as outlined.

Next, I have them work with the theme print they have brought to class and do the same exercise.

Classes in Basic Color Confidence

3 hour class:
Exercises 1, 2, 3, 5, and 7

5 hour class:
Exercises 1, 2, 3, 4, 5, 7, and 8

2 day class:
On the first day, I suggest you teach exercises 1, 2, 3, and 5 and have them vote on quilts (to prepare them for exercise 8). Also the students would be informed at the end of the first class to bring a theme print fabric as well as a variety of prints from their collection to do the texture exercise. On the second day, I suggest you teach exercises 4, 6, 7 and then proceed to exercise 8.

Classes in Palette Practice with Quilts

A 6 session class can be planned after the basic color class is finished to guide students and reinforce the principles that you have taught. Follow steps 1–8 in chapter 6.

RESOURCES

The following supplies and products would be helpful for the student or teacher. If you cannot find them at your local quilt shop, you may order them through Jinny Beyer Studio, P.O. Box 488, Great Falls VA 22066:

- 1" x 3" (2.5cm x 7.6cm) swatches of all 124 PALETTE fabrics
- 6" x 6" (15.2cm x 15.2cm) swatches of all 124 PAL-ETTE fabrics
- Portable Palette®—1 3/4" x 7" (4.5cm x 17.8cm) swatches of the 124 PALETTE fabrics. These swatches are mounted on light weight cardboard and are held together with a screw post. The swatches can be fanned around, moved, and used for creating individual color palettes.
- Portable Palette® refills—24 swatch supplement for those who have a 100 swatch Portable Palette® and want to update it.

Other Jinny Beyer books and videos:

BOOKS: *Patchwork Patterns,* 1979
Quilters Album of Blocks and Borders, 1980
Medallion Quilts, 1982
The Scrap Look, 1985
Patchwork Portfolio, 1989

VIDEOS: *Palettes for Patchwork,* 1987
Mastering Patchwork, 1988
Color Confidence! Concept Videos, 1991

(Except where noted otherwise, all are published by EPM Publications, 1003 Turkey Run Road, Mclean, VA 22101.)

For specific instructions on making quilts and more on color see these other Quilt Digest Press Books:
Color and Cloth, by Mary Coyne Penders
Quilts! Quilts!! Quilts!!!, by Diana McClun and Laura Nownes

Jinny Beyer is an internationally acclaimed quilt-maker, designer, and color expert who for years has shared her love of quilting through her books, videos, teaching, and her masterpiece quilts. Her fabric designs, produced by RJR Fashion Fabrics, are sold throughout the world and have become the trend-setter in the quilting fabric industry.

COLOR SWATCHES AND
SAMPLE MASTER PALETTES

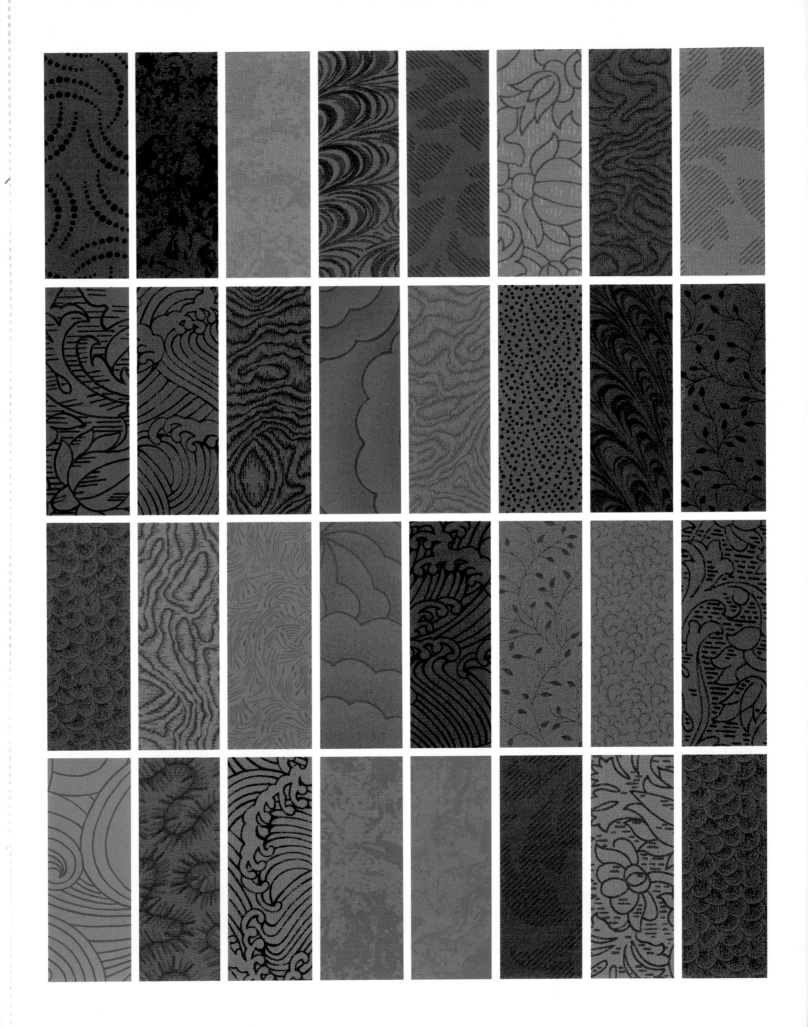

NILE	OLIVE	WEDGWOOD	GINGER	SAFARI	AQUAMARINE	TOBACCO	FOREST
EMERALD	CHESTNUT	AVOCADO	JADE	OCHER	COCOA	AZURE	HEMLOCK
DOVER	BLUE	TURQUOISE	KHAKI	IRIS	CLOVER	ASH	HOLIDAY GREEN
SPRUCE	LAGOON	PINE	CHINESE BLUE	LILAC	SMOKE	PEACOCK	SEA BLUE

INDIGO	ROYAL	BLACK	GRAPE	MEDITER-RANEAN	AMETHYST	SABLE	HYACINTH

LAPIS	EGGPLANT	TWILIGHT	CHARCOAL	BLACKBERRY	CLARET	SAPPHIRE	CYPRESS

COPEN	GARNET	MIDNIGHT	TEAL	COBALT	DEEP SEA	BURGUNDY	TURKEY RED

BRICK	RASPBERRY	PURPLE	CHOCOLATE	MAROON	VIOLET	NAVY	MAGENTA

| YELLOW | MINT | SALMON | DAFFODIL | JASMINE | CARNATION | PALE BLUE | PEACH |

| PEARL | PALOMINO | POWDER BLUE | FOG | SAFFRON | CHIFFON | WHITE | SAND |

| TOPAZ | LEMON | HONEYDEW | ALABASTER | TOFFEE | GLACIER | PINK | BLUSH |

| APPLE GREEN | TAUPE | ICY BLUE | SILVER | AGATE | CELADON | PERIWINKLE | DOGWOOD |

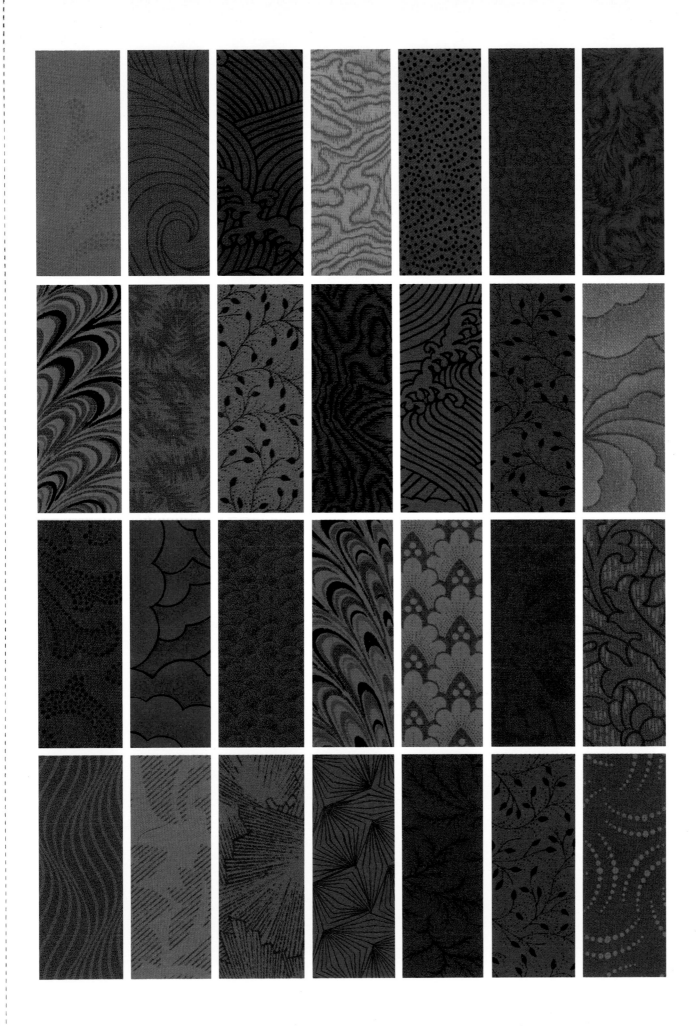

GERANIUM	SCARLET	WATER-MELON	ROSE	CRIMSON	COPPER	PLUM

APRICOT	POPPY	FUCHSIA	RUBY	TEA ROSE	BRONZE	CROCUS

TERRA-COTTA	CINNABAR	ORCHID	REDBUD	PAPRIKA	CARMINE	RUST

PEONY	AZALEA	CHERRY	HENNA	CORAL	MAUVE	BURNT ORANGE

Sample Master Palette 1
Tear along perforation to remove for handy reference.

Sample Master Palette 2
Tear along perforation to remove for handy reference.